REFORM MOVEMENTS
IN AMERICAN
HISTORY

THE
ENVIRONMENTAL
MOVEMENT

PROTECTING OUR NATURAL RESOURCES

The Abolitionist Movement

The Civil Rights Movement

The Environmental Movement

The Ethnic and Group Identity Movements

The Family Values Movement

The Labor Movement

The Progressive Movement

The Women's Rights Movement

THE
ENVIRONMENTAL
MOVEMENT

PROTECTING OUR NATURAL RESOURCES

Liz Sonneborn

Series Editor

Tim McNeese

CHELSEA HOUSE
PUBLISHERS
An imprint of Infobase Publishing

Cover: Environmentalists gather on Capitol Hill during a rally in March 2007 to raise awareness about global warming.

The Environmental Movement: Protecting Our Natural Resources

Copyright © 2008 by Infobase Publishing

Chelsea House
An imprint of Infobase Publishing
132 West 31st Street
New York NY 10001

Library of Congress Cataloging-in-Publication Data
Sonneborn, Liz.
  The environmental movement : protecting our natural resources / Liz Sonneborn.
    p. cm. -- (Reform movements in American history)
  Includes bibliographical references and index.
  ISBN-13: 978-0-7910-9537-9 (hardcover)
  ISBN-10: 0-7910-9537-1 (hardcover)
  1. Environmentalism--United States--History. 2. Social movements--United States--History. I. Title.
  GE197.S66 2007
  333.72--dc22
                              2007014914

Chelsea House books are available at special discounts when purchased in bulk quantities for businesses, associations, institutions, or sales promotions. Please call our Special Sales Department in New York at (212) 967-8800 or (800) 322-8755.

You can find Chelsea House on the World Wide Web at http://www.chelseahouse.com

Series design by Kerry Casey
Cover design by Ben Peterson

Printed in the United States of America

Bang EJB 10 9 8 7 6 5 4 3 2 1

This book is printed on acid-free paper.

All links and Web addresses were checked and verified to be correct at the time of publication. Because of the dynamic nature of the Web, some addresses and links may have changed since publication and may no longer be valid.

CONTENTS

1

Saving the Living World

In 1962, a book invited its readers to imagine an American town "where all life seemed to live in harmony with its surroundings . . . The town lay in the midst of a checkerboard of prosperous farms, with fields of grain and hillsides of orchards, where, in spring white clouds of bloom drifted above the green fields. In autumn, oak and maple and birch set up a blaze of color that flamed and flickered across a backdrop of pines."[1]

Then, suddenly, "a strange blight crept over the area and everything began to change. . . . Everywhere was the shadow of death."[2] The first victims were chickens, then cattle, then sheep. Soon, the farmers and their families became sick with illnesses no doctor could identify. As they began to die, one by one, a "strange stillness"[3] settled over the land. The songbirds that used to fill the air with music all lay dead or dying: "On the mornings that had once throbbed with the dawn chorus of scores of bird voices there was now no sound; only silence lay over the fields and woods and marsh."[4]

With this quiet, death-filled image, scientist and writer Rachel Carson began her book *Silent Spring.* An instant best seller, it would not only make Carson famous. It would also change how Americans looked at themselves and the world around them.

LOVE OF NATURE

To Carson, the combination of writing and science came naturally. A shy girl growing up in western Pennsylvania, she discovered that two of her favorite activities were reading books and going on nature walks. She later attended the Pennsylvania College for Women to study English. In her junior year, however, she took a class in biology that inspired her to concentrate on the study of science. She graduated with a degree in zoology.

After she received a master's degree in zoology from Johns Hopkins University, Carson went to work in the publications department of the U.S. Fish and Wildlife Service. On the side, she began to write articles that presented her vast knowledge of sea life in a clear, often poetic writing style. Carson was disappointed by the low sales of her first book, *Under the Sea-Wind* (1941), but kept writing.

In 1952, her second book, *The Sea Around Us*, was published. To Carson's astonishment, the book was a phenomenal success. Readers responded enthusiastically to her eloquent writing and her passion for the ocean and the living things within it. In just a few months, the book had sold more than 200,000 copies. It earned Carson enough money to buy a house on the coast of Maine, where she could devote all her time to writing.

STUDY OF DDT

Carson went on to write a third book about the ocean, *The Edge of the Sea* (1955), but she was itching to delve into a new subject. Since the mid-1940s, Carson had been interested in writing about dichlorodiphenyltrichloroethane (DDT). Beginning in 1939, the chemical had been used as a pesticide. It was particularly effective at killing mosquitoes, which transmit malaria. Within years, DDT had wiped out this deadly disease in much of the world.

By the 1950s, the Department of Agriculture was routinely distributing DDT to get rid of much less harmful pests. For years, communities across the country were sprayed to destroy caterpillars, moths, and beetles. Some scientists, including Carson, became concerned about this casual use of the pesticide. They worried about the chemical's effect on other living things, including people. Carson became especially alarmed when a friend of hers complained that she found seven dead birds near her house after the area was sprayed with DDT.

Carson began to research the topic, reading scholarly articles and interviewing experts. Although she generally wrote slowly, she had hoped to finish her DDT project quickly. Instead, the work ended up taking four years. Soon after she started the book, she was diagnosed with breast cancer. Her chemotherapy treatments often left her nauseated and bedridden. Despite her ill health, she continued to write, although with a renewed sense of urgency. Carson knew her message about DDT was important. She was determined to bring it to light while she still could.

ON THE ATTACK

Published in book form in September 1962, *Silent Spring* was first excerpted in June 1962 in *The New Yorker* magazine. Carson's work was an immediate sensation. That was hardly surprising, given that, with the success of her earlier books, she already had a built-in audience eager to read her latest work. The book also received some unexpected attention when, soon after *The New Yorker* excerpts appeared, news stories identified a drug called thalidomide as the cause of devastating birth defects. Many readers saw a connection between the disastrous effects of thalidomide and Carson's warnings about DDT, as Carson did herself. She explained, "Thalidomide and pesticides—they represent our willingness to rush ahead

In 1962, Rachel Carson published *Silent Spring*, which detailed the adverse effects pesticides had on the environment, particularly on birds. Carson is pictured here in the library of her Sinking Spring, Maryland, home in 1963.

and use something new without knowing what the results are going to be."[5]

Silent Spring also stayed in the news because of a concerted effort to discredit the book by chemical and agricultural companies that relied on DDT. With the help of the U.S. government, they went on the offensive against Carson and her work. The National Agricultural Chemists Association spent a quarter of a million dollars on a smear campaign. Several companies also spread the idea that the book was written by a hack. Carson was inaccurately criticized as an amateur scientist without professional credentials. Some attacks were more personal, including snide references to her being a "spinster"[6] and accusations that she was a Communist.

Many reporters and critics were equally dismissive. *Life* magazine said Carson "overstated her case."[7] *Time* called her work an "emotional and inaccurate outburst," adding that the book's "scary generalizations—and there are lots of them—are patently unsound."[8]

MAKING HER CASE

In the end, however, the campaign against *Silent Spring* backfired. The more the book was denounced, the more people bought and read it. For months, the book topped the best-seller lists.

Despite her many detractors, the public responded with enthusiasm to Carson's work and her message. With her clean, precise prose, she presented a persuasive case that careless use of DDT posed a threat to the environment and to humans. Carson also made readers question scientists who insisted that DDT was safe without the offer of evidence to back up their position. Perhaps, she told her readers, the scientists did not have enough information to make this claim because they simply had not bothered to examine the possible long-term effects of exposure to DDT and other such chemicals.

The popularity of *Silent Spring* was also due to Carson's calm, refined demeanor. Unexpectedly finding herself in the middle of a highly charged public debate, she responded with care, dignity, and confidence. In April 1963, she appeared on *The Silent Spring of Rachel Carson*—a television show nationally aired on CBS. Before an audience of 15 million, she presented her findings. Carson emphasized that the time had come for humans to end their "conquest" of nature and to recognize that they themselves were part of the natural world. Carson explained, "I think we're challenged, as mankind has never been challenged before, to prove our maturity and our mastery, not of nature but of ourselves."[9]

The next month, Carson was vindicated by a report released by President John F. Kennedy's Science Advisory Committee. Its investigation into DDT supported Carson's conclusions, and the report called for "orderly reductions of persistent pesticides."[10]

CHANGING MINDS

Carson did not live to see the long-term impact of her book. Already weakened by cancer, she died of heart disease on April 14, 1964, at the age of 56. Two years before, just as *Silent Spring* was finding its audience, Carson wrote a friend, describing what she hoped her writing could achieve:

> The beauty of the living world I was trying to save has always been uppermost in my mind—that, and anger at the senseless, brutish things that were being done. I have felt bound by a solemn obligation to do what I could—if I didn't at least try I could never be happy again in nature. But now I can believe that I have at least helped a little. It would be unrealistic to believe one book could bring a complete change.[11]

Carson was correct that her book would help her cause. In 1972, DDT was officially banned in the United States. Although pesticides are still widely used, they are far less toxic than those Carson spoke out against in *Silent Spring.*

Carson, however, was overly modest in doubting that her one book "could bring a complete change." *Silent Spring* did far more than just wake up the public to the dangers

Silent Spring is often credited with helping to get the pesticide DDT (Dichlorodiphenyltrichloroethane) banned in the United States. More importantly, however, Carson's book launched the global environmental movement and changed the way people viewed the natural world.

of pesticides. It also led Americans to reconsider many of their long-held beliefs about the natural world and their place in it. In fact, Carson's greatest legacy is that she sparked a sea change in thought, bringing about a great social and political movement in the United States—the modern environmental movement.

Subdue the Earth

66**S**o God created man in his own image, in the image of God he created him; male and female he created them. And God blessed them, and God said to them, 'Be fruitful and multiply, and fill the earth and subdue it; and have dominion over the fish of the sea and over the birds of the air and over every living thing that moves upon the earth.'"[12] In Genesis 1:27–28, the God of the Old Testament gives these instructions to Adam and Eve.

For the Europeans who began to arrive in North America in the fifteenth century, this biblical command had a special significance. They had risked their lives in the journey across the Atlantic Ocean, drawn by the ample resources offered by what they called the New World. Some came for gold, others for rich farmland, and still others for forests teeming with wildlife. All, however, were determined to "subdue the earth" as the biblical God commanded the first humans to do.

The idea that humans were justified in taking control over the natural world was not found only in Scripture. By the seventeenth century, Europeans were turning increasingly to science to understand their world, and scientific study seemed to reinforce the Bible's notions about man and nature. Scientists of the period generally agreed that humans' ability to reason was evidence of their superiority to the other creatures of the Earth. It easily followed that humans had the right to use their intellect to alter and manipulate nature to suit their needs and desires.

AMERICAN INDIANS AS ENEMIES

Armed with these ideas, Europeans settling in North America tried to make the most of the rich lands there. They farmed soil without the worry of exhausting its nutrients and overhunted animals for meat and fur, unconcerned about their diminishing populations. These settlers also had little regard for the other native inhabitants of their newfound lands—the American Indian peoples who had lived on the continent for centuries.

Although they sometimes killed more buffalo than they needed for food and other uses, American Indians did not harm the environment as much as their European counterparts. Here, renowned American frontier artist George Catlin captures a Plains Indian buffalo hunt in the Upper Missouri River region of the United States.

Europeans assumed they had a right to occupy and dominate the resource-rich lands of North America, but generally they did not extend this right to the Indians they met. In their eyes, Indians had little legitimate claim to the lands they had occupied for generations. As a result, when Europeans found themselves competing with Indians for prime land, they felt justified in the use of force to move Indian peoples from disputed areas.

In these frequent battles, Europeans had an advantage. They possessed guns, which were unknown to Indians before contact with Europeans. With their bows and arrows, Indians were often outmatched by newcomers with these more sophisticated arms.

Unknowingly, the settlers also brought an even more powerful weapon to the Americas: European diseases, such as smallpox and measles. Indians had not previously been exposed to these diseases, so they had no natural immunities to them. Horrible epidemics swept through Indian communities, killing most of the infected. To many European colonists, these mass deaths provided evidence that God intended them to be the sole possessors and masters of the New World. For example, after a 1634 epidemic, John Winthrop, a leader of England's Massachusetts Bay Colony, wrote, "For the natives they are neere all dead of small Poxe, so as the Lord hathe cleared our title to what we possess."[13]

CELEBRATING THE SPIRITS

Like Europeans, American Indians had religious ideas about the place of humans in nature. Unlike Europeans, though, they generally wanted to live in harmony with the natural world rather than to subdue it to their will. The spiritual beliefs of Indians differed from tribe to tribe and from region to region, yet many groups shared a reverence for plants and animals and believed in spiritual beings who protected the natural world. Not surprisingly, Indian peoples often held seasonal rituals to thank the spirits for important foods that nature provided. For instance, in the Pacific Northwest, many groups performed a ritual to celebrate the beginning of the spring salmon run, whereas in the Southeast, many tribes held a ceremony to express appreciation for that year's corn crop.

Because of such rituals and beliefs, in recent years Indians have been praised as America's first environmentalists. In truth, however, Indians were sometimes just as careless about exploiting the natural world as non-Indians. Like Europeans, those living in areas rich in resources could not imagine that these resources would ever run out. For instance, in areas with fertile farmland, many Indian groups routinely destroyed land through overfarming, secure in the knowledge that they could simply move their fields to fertile areas nearby. In western lands, where large numbers of buffalo existed, Indian hunters often drove herds over cliffs. In this way, hunting allowed them to kill many buffalo with fairly little effort. In fact, the kills were often so spectacular that the hunters, with far more dead prey than they could use, left a pile of rotting corpses behind.

In this light, Indians cannot be seen as environmentalists, in the modern sense of the word. They made minimal effort to conserve resources where they were plentiful and would never have considered preserving wilderness areas for their own sake. Instead, they merely sought the best way to live within their surroundings. Those who lived in desert lands or other areas with few resources carefully maintained and conserved what they had. Those who were surrounded by lush farmland or forests filled with wild animals discovered ways to make the most of these resources with as little work as possible.

DAMAGING THE LANDSCAPE

Differences between Indians and Europeans in terms of the impact they had on the land, however, were evident. Even when Indians were careless in their use of natural resources, they caused fairly little lasting damage. Before contact with the Europeans, their populations were too small, and their land base too large, to have a major effect on the environment. After contact, their numbers plummeted from disease and warfare, further reducing their impact on the land.

The effect of European and later American settlement, however, was much greater. As their settlements became more established, their populations grew quickly, forcing more and more people to compete for resources. The strain on the land was often so great that people had to leave their communities for areas that were less populated. In fact, one of the most significant features of the early history of the United States was this constant movement, especially to lands west of the original 13 American colonies.

Non-Indians also introduced technologies to the continent that were both more advanced and more destructive than those used by Indian peoples. Guns, for example, allowed settlers to hunt more effectively, even to the point of driving some species to near extinction. This happened to the American beaver in the early nineteenth century, when a vogue for beaver hats in Europe made fortunes for a few fur trappers and traders. Metal tools were another technological innovation that left a mark on the land. They allowed non-Indian farmers to clear and cultivate increasingly larger plots of land, without regard for any longer-term consequences on the environment.

Non-Indians also brought new species of plants and animals to North America. Immigrants, sometimes unknowingly, introduced seeds of European plants that overtook and destroyed native varieties. They carried over European animals, such as cattle, sheep, and horses. Although these animals were beneficial to non-Indians and Indians alike, in some areas they drove off native animals, such as deer and antelope. By the alteration of these native animals' territories and populations, the newcomers forever changed the continent's landscape.

RETHINKING NATURE

In early America, most people ignored the ways humans were changing nature. If they noticed these changes at all, they were unconcerned, considering it a small price to pay for human progress.

By the early nineteenth century, however, some intellectuals started to think that humans should show greater respect toward the natural world. In Europe, these ideas spawned the romantic movement. Romantic painters, writers, and philosophers celebrated the spiritual power of nature and questioned mankind's supposed superiority over other forms of life.

By the mid-nineteenth century, in the United States, romanticism helped inspire transcendentalism. This literary and cultural movement held that people could have direct experience with the spiritual realm without the help of an organized religion. For the transcendentalists, the contemplation and appreciation of nature was a particularly rewarding means to elevate the spirit and transcend the everyday world.

The most well-known transcendentalist was Ralph Waldo Emerson. A noted essayist and lecturer, Emerson's collection of essays *Nature* (1836) had a great influence on American intellectuals of the day. In this work, Emerson wrote of nature's spiritual power:

American essayist and poet Ralph Waldo Emerson was the leader of the transcendentalist movement, which espoused that people did not need organized religion to connect to the spiritual realm. In 1836, Emerson published his most famous work, *Nature*, a collection of essays that detailed the spiritual power of nature.

In the woods, we return to reason and faith. There I feel that nothing can befall me in life—no disgrace, no calamity (leaving me my eyes,) which nature cannot repair. Standing on the bare ground—my head bathed by the blithe air, and uplifted into infinite space—all mean egotism vanishes. I become a transparent eyeball; I am nothing; I see all; the currents of the Universal Being circulate through me; I am part or particle of God.[14]

Emerson befriended a young writer named Henry David Thoreau. In 1845, Emerson offered Thoreau the use of a plot of land he owned near Walden Pond in Massachusetts. There, Thoreau lived alone for two years in a small house he built on the property. He chronicled his experiences, especially his attempts to live in harmony with nature, in his book *Walden* (1854). Although not widely read in his lifetime, the memoir eventually became an inspirational text for later generations of American environmentalists.

Another important writer of the time was George Perkins Marsh. A lawyer and noted linguist, Marsh became fascinated with the effect of humans on the environment. In his book *Man and Nature: Or, Physical Geography as Modified by Human Action* (1864), he spoke out against society's uncontrolled growth, warning that it could lead to the destruction of forests, waterways, and the wildlife they sustained. Now considered a classic of environmental literature, Marsh's book concluded that "man is everywhere a disturbing agent"[15] and urged countries around the world to take immediate action to lessen the damage humans were inflicting on the Earth.

IGNORING SIGNS

The ideas of Emerson, Thoreau, and Marsh received attention in intellectual circles. Their cautions about mankind's exploitation of nature gained little ground, however, with the broader public. After all, by the mid-nineteenth century, Americans had seen their country grow enormously through the purchase of land from other countries and by the seizure

ON WALDEN POND

In his lifetime, writer and philosopher Henry David Thoreau (1817–1862) published relatively little. Two of his works, however, would have a profound influence on later American social movements. His essay "Civil Disobedience" (1849) inspired Martin Luther King Jr. and his followers in the civil rights movement of the 1950s and 1960s. His book *Walden* (1854) emerged as a central text for the environmental movement that matured during the 1970s. In *Walden*, Thoreau described his personal experiment of living alone in the wilderness, an experience that led him to contemplate the proper relationship between humans and nature.

In the following excerpt from "The Ponds" chapter of *Walden*, Thoreau describes how, despite human desecration of the area around Walden Pond, the landscape remained for him "perennially young":

> When I first paddled a boat on Walden, it was completely surrounded by thick and lofty pine and oak woods, and in some of its coves grape vines had run over the trees next to the water and formed bowers under which a boat could pass. The hills which form its shores are so steep, and the woods on them were then so high, that, as you looked down from the west end, it had the appearance of an amphitheatre for some kind of sylvan spectacle. I have spent many an hour, when I was younger, floating over its surface as the zephyr willed, having paddled my boat to the middle, and lying on my back across the seats, in a

of territory from Mexico and from Indian tribes. For most Americans, accustomed to an expanding nation, it seemed as though the country would always have enough land.

As the United States grew, so did the belief of Americans that the country's prosperity was God's will. The popular term *manifest destiny* embodied the idea that God wanted the nation to stretch all the way from the Atlantic Ocean to the Pacific Ocean. In the American mind, the acquisition of summer forenoon, dreaming awake, until I was aroused by the boat touching the sand, and I arose to see what shore my fates had impelled me to; days when idleness was the most attractive and productive industry. . . .

Now the trunks of trees on the bottom, and the old log canoe, and the dark surrounding woods, are gone. . . .

Nevertheless, of all the characters I have known, perhaps Walden wears best, and best preserves its purity. Many men have been likened to it, but few deserve that honor. Though the woodchoppers have laid bare first this shore and then that, and the Irish have built their sties by it, and the railroad has infringed on its border, and the ice-men have skimmed it once, it is itself unchanged, the same water which my youthful eyes fell on; all the change is in me. It has not acquired one permanent wrinkle after all its ripples. It is perennially young, and I may stand and see a swallow dip apparently to pick an insect from its surface as of yore. It struck me again tonight, as if I had not seen it almost daily for more than twenty years,—Why, here is Walden, the same woodland lake that I discovered so many years ago; where a forest was cut down last winter another is springing up by its shore as lustily as ever.* . . .

* Henry David Thoreau, *Walden and Other Writings of Henry David Thoreau*; repr. (New York: Modern Library, 1937), 173–174.

this land came with an obligation to God to use it and its resources for America's benefit.

In the second half of the nineteenth century, the country's exploitation of its resources accelerated. The American population was growing quickly, with the aid of immigration. As their numbers increased, the American people required more food and goods, and industries expanded to satisfy this demand. As manufacturing and agricultural businesses grew, the need for raw materials to produce food, create goods, and fuel factories became more urgent than ever. To help satisfy this need, new machinery and technologies were developed. Now, industry could cut down forests, dam waterways, and mine minerals faster than before. At the same time, factories, burning wood and coal, sent clouds of filthy smoke into the air and poured industrial waste products into the water.

The U.S. government did little to control industry's use of resources. In fact, some government policies encouraged corporations to exploit them recklessly. For instance, legislation such as the Timber Act of 1873 made it easier for large companies to gain access to government lands and extract their resources at little cost and without supervision by authority.

The transcontinental railroad, completed in 1869, also sped the growth of industry. Railroads allowed for easy transport of food and goods, which in turn enabled people to concentrate in cities. Life in crowded urban areas was new to many Americans. Not long before, nearly all Americans had lived and worked on farms. In rural areas, they were well acquainted with the rhythms of nature and the need for proper care of fields and livestock. Just about every object they used—from beds to baskets to bowls—they crafted themselves from natural materials. In the city, on the other hand, Americans relied on food and products grown, processed, or made hundreds or even thousands of miles away. Unlike their ancestors, these Americans no longer had to struggle to conquer the natural world. In fact, those confined to the nation's bustling cities could easily live their lives with almost no contact with nature at all.

3

Early Stirrings

By the end of the nineteenth century, the United States had become a global power. It was a prosperous nation, with many of its citizens enjoying a quality of life that would have been unimaginable just a generation before.

In 1893, however, a noted historian named Frederick Jackson Turner warned that America's uniqueness and greatness faced a new threat. Before an audience at the American Historical Society, he quoted a U.S. Census report from 1890. It said that "up to and including 1880 the country had a frontier of settlement, but at present the unsettled area has been so broken into by isolated bodies of settlement that there can hardly be said to be a frontier line."[16]

For Turner, this fading of the frontier, which he called "the meeting point of savagery and civilization,"[17] had important consequences for the country. The historian maintained that the character of Americans—their strength and sense of individualism—came from their experiences in taking control over frontier lands. As the frontier closed, so "closed the first period of American history."[18] Turner's essay suggested a question: In the next period of American history, without a wilderness to conquer, would Americans be able to retain the traits that had allowed them to thrive?

Turner's theory was much discussed in intellectual circles. The loss of wilderness lands also posed more immediate and concrete challenges—challenges that greater numbers of Americans were beginning to acknowledge. Decades of unbridled exploitation of nature were starting to take their toll. Overfarming on the Great Plains was destroying the soil there. Mining coal, iron ore, copper, and gold had created permanent scars on the land in mineral-rich regions. Wood was becoming scarce as America's forests were destroyed by the timber industry. As a replacement for wood, coal was increasingly burned as fuel, which further polluted the air.

In the past, Americans could afford to be careless in their treatment of the environment. After all, when people exhausted resources in one area, they could always move to another. Now, however, with few unsettled areas left in the country, there was nowhere to escape to. Slowly, public and political leaders came to realize that, even in the United States, land was precious, and its resources could not necessarily be replaced.

JOHN MUIR'S VISION

By the beginning of the twentieth century, these new concerns about the environment had sparked a back-to-nature movement. Many Americans, especially city dwellers, sought spiritual and emotional fulfillment by spending leisure time in wilderness areas. Particularly popular were national and state parks. Between 1908 and 1915, attendance rose nearly 500 percent. People also encouraged their children to experience nature. The Boy Scouts and Girl Scouts were founded to foster children's civic and moral development through outdoor adventures.

As part of this movement, artists began to create nature scenes, and authors turned to nature writing. The most popular of these writers was John Muir. Muir established the Sierra Club in 1892. As the organization's president, he spoke out against the massive growth of industry in the United States. He saw industrial America as a soulless destroyer of nature and the spiritual force it contained. Muir believed wilderness areas needed to be protected by laws that prohibited any use of their resources by business concerns.

Like Muir, some people in the political arena had begun to question unregulated business growth. They referred to themselves as Progressives, and the period of their political prominence (approximately from 1900 to 1920) became known as the Progressive Era.

The growth of industry had certainly increased the nation's wealth. In the Progressives' view, however, it also had created serious problems in American society, including crowded, dirty urban areas and a disturbing gap between the incomes of the poorest and richest citizens. The Progressives believed that the government, if well managed, could help solve these problems by the use of laws and regulations to rein in the worst excesses of American industry.

One of the primary goals of Progressive politics was the conservation of America's natural resources. Progressives believed that government bureaucrats, armed with scientific and technical training, should set down rules for land and resource management. The Progressives did not want to stifle industry or reduce its access to necessary resources. Instead, they wanted to ensure that corporations used resources more responsibly so that they would still be available for generations to come.

CONSERVATIONIST PRESIDENT

The leading Progressive conservationist was Republican politician Theodore Roosevelt. Elected vice president in 1900, he became the youngest American president after the death of President William McKinley the following year. Roosevelt was well known as an outdoorsman and took pride in his exploits as a hunter and fisherman.

"ONLY UNCLE SAM CAN DO THAT"

Born in Scotland in 1838, John Muir at 11 years of age moved to Wisconsin, where his family established a farm. As a young man, Muir was temporary blinded and traveled to San Francisco, California, for treatment. When his eyesight was restored, he became enraptured by the California landscape, particularly the forests of stately redwood trees in the Yosemite Valley. With wonder and passion, he wrote numerous books and magazine articles about Yosemite, inspiring his readers to campaign for the preservation of this and other wilderness areas.

The following excerpt, from Muir's book *Our National Parks* (1901), explains the role he believed the federal government should play in the preservation of the nation's natural treasures:

> The United States government has always been proud of the welcome it has extended to good men of every nation, seeking freedom and homes and bread. Let them be welcomed still as nature welcomes them, to the woods as well as to the prairies and plains. Let them be as free to pick gold and gems from the hills, to cut and hew, dig and plant, for homes and bread, as the birds are to pick berries from the wild bushes, and moss and leaves for nests. Mere destroyers, however, tree-killers, wool and mutton men, spreading death and confusion in the fairest groves and gardens ever planted—let the government hasten to cast them out and make an end of them. For it must be told again and again, and be burningly borne in mind, that just now, while protective measures are being deliberated languidly, destruction and use are speeding on faster and farther every day. The axe and saw are insanely busy, chips are flying thick as snowflakes, and every summer thousands of acres of priceless forests, with

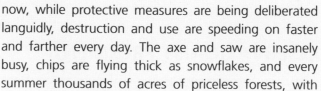

Not surprisingly, he was also an admirer of John Muir. In 1903, Roosevelt accompanied Muir on a visit to the Yosemite Valley. For three days, the two men wandered through the

their underbrush, soil, springs, climate, scenery, and religion, are vanishing away in clouds of smoke, while, except in the national parks, not one forest guard is employed.

All sorts of local laws and regulations have been tried and found wanting, and the costly lessons of our own experience, as well as that of every civilized nation, show conclusively that the fate of the remnant of our forests is in the hands of the federal government, and that if the remnant is to be saved at all, it must be saved quickly.

Any fool can destroy trees. They cannot run away; and if they could, they would still be destroyed—chased and hunted down as long as fun or a dollar could be got out of their bark hides, branching horns, or magnificent bole backbones. Few that fell trees plant them; nor would planting avail much towards getting back anything like the noble primeval forests. During a man's life only saplings can be grown, in the place of the old trees—tens of centuries old—that have been destroyed. It took more than three thousand years to make some of the trees in these Western woods, trees that are still standing in perfect strength and beauty, waving and singing in the mighty forests of the Sierra. Through all the wonderful, eventful centuries since Christ's time—and long before that God has cared for these trees, saved them from drought, disease, avalanches, and a thousand straining, leveling tempests and floods; but he cannot save them from fools, only Uncle Sam can do that.*

* John Muir, *Our National Parks*. Sierra Club. Available online at *http://www.sierraclub.org/john_muir_exhibit/frameindex. html?http://www.sierraclub.org/john_muir_exhibit/writings/our_ national_parks/chapter_10.html.*

The founder and first president of the Sierra Club, John Muir believed that wilderness areas needed to be preserved and that businesses should be forbidden from using their resources. Muir (right) is pictured here in 1903 with President Theodore Roosevelt at Glacier Point in California's Yosemite National Park.

great redwood forests, camping under the stars once night fell. After their trip, Roosevelt joined Muir's successful campaign to bring the valley, then controlled by the state of California, under the protection of the federal government.

Throughout his presidency, Roosevelt was a staunch proponent of conservation, referring to it as "my policy."[19] During his tenure, the federal government added 130 million acres to its national forests and established 51 areas as national wildlife refuges. Roosevelt also pushed for important legislation, such as the Newlands Reclamation Act of 1902, which helped fund dams and canals to assist in the regulation of water use across the country.

In Roosevelt's eyes, conservation was not a threat to the wealth of the nation, as some industrialists suggested. Instead, he argued, conservation was necessary if the U.S. economy were to continue to grow. As Roosevelt explained, "It is safe to say that the prosperity of our people depends directly on the energy and intelligence with which our natural resources are used."[20]

CONSERVATION VERSUS PRESERVATION

Roosevelt's most important ally in promoting conservation was Gifford Pinchot. Greatly influenced by the writings of George Perkins Marsh, Pinchot headed to Europe to study forestry, because at the time no American institution offered training in that field. After he returned to the United States, Pinchot was appointed chief forester of the United States. In 1905, Roosevelt tapped Pinchot to head the United States Forest Service.

Like Roosevelt, Pinchot was a conservationist. He believed that the country's natural resources should be used, but that their use should be regulated—not by for-profit companies, but by professionally trained government employees who had no direct financial stake in the businesses involved. Pinchot's position earned him the scorn of some business owners, especially in the West, who thought their companies should be free to use resources however they saw fit without government interference. They disparaged his ideas, which they branded as Pinchotism.

Pinchot also drew wrath from Muir and other preservationists, who were leery of Pinchot's conservation policies. They felt a moral calling to protect natural areas from exploitation. Nature and its resources should be preserved for their own sake, not conserved just so that humankind could take advantage of them more efficiently and effectively. Muir's Sierra Club appreciated that Pinchot's work might prevent the worst destruction of wilderness areas. Its members feared, however, that, by allowing industry to make use of these areas at all, Pinchot might, in fact, help businesses damage them further.

Pinchot was equally suspicious of Muir and his followers. As a conservationist, he wished to make proper use of land, not leave it untouched, as preservationists wanted. In May 1908, Roosevelt organized the Governors' Conference on the Conservation of Natural Resources at the White House. The first conference of its kind in the United States, it brought together hundreds of governors, industrialists, scientists, and members of Congress to discuss the federal government's environmental policy. One notable expert was missing, however. Pinchot had made sure Muir was not invited.

THE HETCH HETCHY PROJECT

The battle between Pinchot and Muir came to a head in 1913. For several years, the government had been weighing a proposal to dam the Tuolumne River in northern California. The river ran through the Hetch Hetchy Valley, which was included in lands the U.S. government had designated as Yosemite National Park, the first national park, in 1872.

The dam would create a great reservoir, thereby solving a long-standing problem: San Francisco desperately needed a large, reliable source of water. The dam would also make it possible to use the river water to create electricity, providing power to the growing city.

Muir's Sierra Club came out strongly against the Hetch Hetchy Dam. The organization charged that the dam would destroy the valley's natural beauty for all time. Muir spearheaded an aggressive national campaign and

In the early 1900s, the Sierra Club opposed the U.S. government's proposed construction of the Hetch Hetchy Dam, which Muir and his organization felt would damage Yosemite's natural beauty. The Hetch Hetchy Valley was formed by glaciers 10,000 years ago and is pictured here prior to the dam's construction.

wrote many articles and letters demanding that the Hetch Hetchy be saved. With characteristic passion, Muir wrote to Oregon senator George E. Chamberlain, who was serving as chairman of the Committee on Geological Survey: "In behalf of all the people of the nation we ask your aid in putting an end to these assaults on our great national parks and to prevent this measure from being rushed through before it can be brought to the attention of the ninety millions of people who own this park."[21]

Muir's argument failed to convince Gifford Pinchot or even his old friend Teddy Roosevelt, who had left the presidency in 1909. They both promoted the dam project, insisting that it would not only help provide drinking water for San Francisco but also create a recreational area that all Americans could enjoy. With Roosevelt's full support, a bill calling for the dam was passed by Congress and signed into law on December 13, 1913.

Losing the battle for the Hetch Hetchy was devastating to John Muir. Deeply saddened and physically weak, Muir died of pneumonia the next year at the age of 76. Despite their disagreements over the Hetch Hetchy project, Roosevelt wrote an essay for *Outlook* magazine to commemorate his old friend, concluding, "Our generation owes much to John Muir."[22]

In his final fight for the California wilderness, Muir had failed. The battle he and his followers waged, however, revealed an important shift in American attitudes toward the environment. Through their efforts, the dam project had been the subject of a national debate—one that would have been inconceivable only a few decades before. After the Hetch Hetchy controversy, it became clear that, even when Americans favored economic progress over preservationist ideals, they were now at least willing to take both sides seriously.

4

An Emerging Movement

As the Progressive Era faded, so did the attention paid to conservation. The administrations that followed Roosevelt's were more concerned with protecting business interests than with protecting the environment. They were generally uninterested in passing new conservation legislation or even in enforcing laws set in place by Progressives.

The public, too, was distracted from environmental concerns. During the 1920s, Americans were enjoying an economic boom, which allowed them to indulge their fascination with the latest consumer goods. More and more people could afford automobiles and electrical appliances. In that decade, use of electricity rose by more than 300 percent. Cars burning gasoline and power plants fueled by oil and coal sent clouds of noxious smoke into the air. For most Americans, though, that was a small price to pay for the marvels of electricity and the automobile.

THE NEW DEAL

Although interest in environmental issues ebbed during this period, it never went away completely. The Sierra Club continued to gain membership. Other environmental groups also thrived. They included the Audubon Society (founded in 1905), the Izaak

Walton League (1922), the Wilderness Society (1935), and the National Wildlife Federation (1936).

In the 1930s, conservation also found strong support in the White House. Democratic president Franklin D. Roosevelt, who served from 1933 to 1945, initiated a series of programs called the New Deal to help combat poverty during the Great Depression. Among these programs was the Civilian Conservation Corps (CCC). The CCC hired young, unemployed Americans, including teenagers, to work on a variety of conservation projects. CCC employees

THE LAND ETHIC

Aldo Leopold (1887–1948) served in the U.S. Forest Service for 19 years, helped found the Wilderness Society, and spent his final years as a professor of game management at the University of Wisconsin. Those achievements alone would have made him one of the leading environmentalists of his time. Leopold today is best known, however, as the author of *A Sand County Almanac*, now considered a classic of environmental literature. The book was published in 1949, a year after Leopold died of a heart attack while fighting a brush fire.

The final and most famous chapter in *A Sand County Almanac* is titled "The Land Ethic." As the excerpt below explains, Leopold believed that land, and the animal and plant life it sustains, has an ethical standing, a right to be as important as humankind's right to be:

All ethics so far evolved rest upon a single premise: that the individual is a member of a community of interdependent parts. His instincts prompt him to compete for his place in the community, but his ethics prompt him also to cooperate (perhaps in order that there may be a place to compete for).

The land ethic simply enlarges the boundaries of the community to include soils, waters, plants, and animals, or collectively: the land.

constructed trails and tourist lodges in national and state parks, labored on projects to suppress forest fires and prevent soil erosion, and planted billions of trees. Roosevelt also supported legislation to improve the water supply and regulate use of farmlands. His administration expanded the national park system and established the U.S. Fish and Wildlife Service in 1939.

Roosevelt's environmental record was impressive, but still many preservationists thought he did not do enough. They rightly noted that Roosevelt, facing the challenge

This sounds simple: do we not already sing our love for and obligation to the land of the free and the home of the brave? Yes, but just what and whom do we love? Certainly not the soil, which we are sending helter-skelter downriver. Certainly not the waters, which we assume have no function except to turn turbines, float barges, and carry off sewage. Certainly not the plants, of which we exterminate whole communities without batting an eye. Certainly not the animals, of which we have already extirpated many of the largest and most beautiful species. A land ethic of course cannot prevent the alteration, management, and use of these "resources," but it does affirm their right to continued existence, and, at least in spots, their continued existence in a natural state.

In short, a land ethic changes the role of Homo sapiens from conqueror of the land-community to plain member and citizen of it. It implies respect for his fellow-members, and also respect for the community as such.*

* Aldo Leopold, *A Sand County Almanac*, repr. (New York: Ballantine Books, 1966), 239–240.

of strengthening the country's faltering economy, was reluctant to take any measures that could threaten economic growth.

FAITH IN SCIENCE

After the United States entered World War II (1939–1945) in 1941, environmental policy was again placed on the back burner. Americans were first focused on the war. Then, following their victory, they were preoccupied with the reestablishment of order in their lives. The outcome of the war and the economic boom that followed gave Americans a new confidence. They championed industrial expansion and progress, even if it threatened the environment. After all, if they had helped win a world war, they could surely undo any short-term environmental damage over the long haul.

Many Americans of the post–World War II era placed enormous faith in technology and science. Recent advances suggested that science could find a solution to any difficulty, including environmental problems caused by the irresponsible use of land and resources. It was just this confidence in scientific progress that helped popularize the pesticide DDT that Rachel Carson condemned in her book *Silent Spring.* Between 1947 and 1960, the United States increased its annual production of the DDT from 124 million pounds to 637 million pounds.

GROWING FEARS

Not everyone, however, was comfortable with the post–World War II world. Many people were overwhelmed by anxiety over the wartime invention of the atomic bomb. The U.S. Army dropped the bomb on the Japanese cities of Hiroshima and Nagasaki in August 1945. An estimated 200,000 people died from the blast or from the radioactivity it unleashed. The atomic bomb horrified many Americans,

In addition to the 200,000 people who died in the bombing of Hiroshima and Nagasaki at the end of World War II, radioactivity from the atomic blast destroyed much of the flora and fauna of southern Japan. This photo taken by the Army Signal Corps shortly after the first bomb was dropped on Hiroshima on August 6, 1945, reveals the devastation such a blast can cause.

especially after the powerful Soviet Union developed its own nuclear weapons. For those terrified of nuclear war, scientific progress hardly seemed like the savior of humanity. Instead, science had created a weapon so powerful that it could destroy the Earth.

Some Americans were also uneasy with the direction being taken by their society. After the war, many people just wanted to live a comfortable life with access to as many material comforts as possible. They moved to suburban areas, spending greater amounts of time in their cars as they commuted long distances from the house to the workplace. They spent their extra income on a wide array of new products, many made of new plastic materials and sold in elaborate packaging. These new ways were supposed to represent the good life, but many found this way of life unsatisfying. Some people became deeply concerned about materialism—constant obsession with the latest products and gadgets that created more garbage as old things were thrown away to make room for the new ones. They were disturbed by the pollution, litter, and damaged landscapes they saw around them. As John C. Whitaker, undersecretary of the Department of the Interior between 1973 and 1975, later explained: "As Americans traveled in their automobiles, which had doubled in number from 1950 to 1970, they saw garish road signs, fields of junked automobiles, choked and dying streams, overgrazed and eroded hills and valleys, and roadsides lined with endless miles of beer cans, pop bottles, and the tin foil from candy wrappers and cigarette packages."[23]

It was because of these concerns that Carson's *Silent Spring* became such a cultural phenomenon. Before her book, few Americans knew much about DDT. Many were already thinking, however, of the dangers in placing too much faith in science and too much emphasis on material things. *Silent Spring* only confirmed what its readers suspected: Americans needed to sit up and pay attention to what their lifestyle was doing to the planet.

THE WILDERNESS ACT

Politicians in Washington, D.C., certainly noticed the reawakened interest in environmental issues. It was particularly obvious from the public reaction to a bill designed to protect federally owned wilderness areas from development that had been debated in Congress since the late 1950s. The bill was championed by conservationist Howard Clinton Zahniser, the executive secretary of the Wilderness Society. Despite

Zahniser's lobbying, the bill initially went nowhere, as it faced broad opposition by commercial interests and legislators from several western states.

Then, environmental groups and mainstream organizations, including the Federation of Women's Clubs, took up the cause. Members wrote to lawmakers of their enthusiastic support for the bill. By 1962, Congress was receiving more letters about the wilderness bill than any other subject. The public pressure finally compelled Congress to pass the bill into law in September 1964.

The Wilderness Act was a landmark in environmental legislation. It created a legal definition for the word *wilderness:* "An area where the earth and its community of life are untrammeled by man, where man himself is a visitor who does not remain."[24] The act also established the National Wilderness Preservation System, which eventually preserved and protected the wildlife on more than 100 million acres of federal land. Once a place was designated as an official wilderness area, only an act of Congress could remove this protection.

The administrations of John F. Kennedy and Lyndon B. Johnson recognized the popularity of environmental legislation and policy. Under President Kennedy, the federal government increased funding for national parks, and Congress passed the Clean Air Act (1963), which earmarked money for combating air pollution. Johnson's administration held a White House Conference on Natural Beauty in May 1965. Several months before, President Johnson sent to Congress a special message calling for "a new conservation" that concerned itself with natural beauty not just in wilderness areas but also in cities:

> To deal with these new problems will require a new conservation. We must not only protect the countryside and save it from destruction, we must restore what has

been destroyed and salvage the beauty and charm of our cities. . . . Its concern is not with nature alone, but with the total relation between man and the world around him. Its object is not just man's welfare but the dignity of man's spirit.[25]

Aside from the Wilderness Act, little real progress was made in environmental legislation during the Johnson administration. As first lady, Claudia "Lady Bird" Johnson, however, did promote the Highway Beautification Act (1965), which called for decorative landscaping and a reduction of billboards along roadsides.

REVAMPING THE SIERRA CLUB

Like the federal government, older environmental groups took note of the new public interest in environmentalism. In the past, the bulk of their membership was made up of older, fairly wealthy Americans who had the money, time, and leisure to take part in outdoor sports and activities. As more Americans, especially young people, became involved in the movement, however, the established organizations tried to attract new members by embracing new causes. For instance, the Audubon Society, dedicated to the conservation of wildlife habitats, became involved in the fight against DDT, and the Izaak Walton League, originally an organization for outdoorsmen, began to campaign for clean water laws.

These organizations also started to adopt new techniques to reach the public and push their agendas. Especially noteworthy were the efforts of the Sierra Club under the leadership of David Brower. Brower served as the organization's executive director from 1952 to 1969. His Sierra Club produced many articles and books, including several illustrated by photographer Ansel Adams, who was famed for his popular black-and-white nature scenes. This

David Brower served as the executive director of the Sierra Club from 1952 to 1969. During his tenure, Brower established a publishing branch that not only helped the Sierra Club educate the general public on environmental concerns but also brought in millions of dollars to help fund its programs.

publishing program eventually brought millions of dollars into the organization. Brower also used lectures and films to spread the Sierra Club's message even further.

In the mid-1960s, Brower focused his talent for generating publicity on a battle to prevent the U.S. government's Bureau of Reclamation from building two dams on the Colorado River in the Grand Canyon. The Sierra Club took out a series of full-page newspaper advertisements to explain its campaign. The text denouncing the government plan declared, "This time it's the Grand Canyon they want to flood. *The Grand Canyon*,"[26] and offered suggestions for how concerned citizens could write to their congressmen to express their opposition. The Sierra Club also distributed bumper stickers and pamphlets and issued a book showing the glories of the Grand Canyon in lush photos.

Letters and phone calls flooded into Congress. Magazines and newspapers picked up the story, further spreading the word about the Sierra Club's fight. The campaign worked. By the late 1960s, the federal government gave up its plan to dam the Colorado. The government took revenge on the Sierra Club by revoking its tax-exempt status, making it more difficult for the organization to raise funds. Nevertheless, the Sierra Club prospered as its membership soared from 39,000 in 1966 to 113,000 in 1970.

NEW LEADERS, NEW GOALS

While traditional organizations were beginning to change their focus and tactics, brand-new organizations and leaders emerged. One such leader was Ralph Nader. A Washington lawyer, Nader wrote *Unsafe at Any Speed* (1965), an exposé of the lack of safety standards in the automobile industry. Inspired by Nader's willingness to battle huge corporations, a group of young activists nicknamed Nader's Raiders joined Nader to take on a number of causes, including several environmental issues. For instance, Nader and his followers used lawsuits against corporations and government agencies to fight air pollution, water contamination, and toxic chemical dumps. Nader's work revealed that the courtroom could be an effective arena for waging environmental battles.

Another influential figure was Paul Ehrlich. Ehrlich was a professor of biology at Stanford University when he wrote an article about overpopulation for *New Scientist* magazine. At David Brower's urging, Ehrlich expanded the article into a book, *The Population Bomb* (1968). In the past, other scientists had warned that, as the world population grew, humans would eventually place an unsustainable stress on the Earth and its resources. However, *The Population Bomb,* written with a general audience in mind, was the first book to present this idea to a mass audience. More than 3 million copies were in print by the end of the next decade. Ehrlich also helped to found Zero Population Growth, an organization devoted to raising awareness of the dangers of overpopulation and to promoting birth control and family planning.

Another biologist, Barry Commoner, sounded a persuasive warning about the impact of technology on the environment. In the 1950s, Commoner spoke out against the nuclear weapons tests performed by the United States and Soviet Union, charging that they were unleashing dangerous amounts of radioactivity. His efforts and those of other like-minded scientists led to the Nuclear Test Ban Treaty of 1963. To further his work, Commoner helped found the Committee for Nuclear Information, which was renamed the Committee for Environmental Information after the organization decided to broaden its focus to a host of environmental issues. Renowned for his ability to communicate complex scientific information to the layperson, Barry Commoner was hailed as the "Paul Revere" of environmentalism in a glowing profile in *Time* magazine in 1970.

By the end of the 1960s, Americans' concerns about the environment had transformed into a full-fledged movement. After a period of complacency in the early twentieth century, *Silent Spring* brought environmental issues to the forefront of American culture and politics. In just a few years, the movement grew at an amazing rate. Not only did more people become involved in environmentalism but also the concerns of the movement expanded well beyond the conservation of wilderness areas to embrace newer issues such as air pollution, nuclear dangers, and overpopulation. The expansion of the movement during the 1960s had indeed been startling, but its greatest growth was yet to come. Only after America entered the "green decade" of the 1970s would the true power of environmentalism in American society become clear.

5

The Green Decade

On April 22, 1970, it was warm and sunny throughout much of the United States. Many Americans gathered in parks, on college campus greens, in schoolyards, and on city sidewalks. They were not just there to enjoy the beautiful spring weather. They came together to celebrate a national event—the country's first Earth Day.

Some spent the day planting trees and cleaning up litter. Others held parades or attended rallies. Still others staged protests to dramatize the goals of environmentalism. In Tacoma, Washington, about 100 students rode horses down a highway to speak out against pollution-causing auto emissions. In San Francisco, California, a group calling itself the Environmental Vigilantes poured oil into a reflecting pool outside the corporate offices of the Standard Oil Company to draw attention to destructive oil spills. In New York City, protestors marched down Fifth Avenue, holding up dead fish to symbolize the polluting of the nearby Hudson River.

Approximately 20 million Americans took part in these and hundreds of other events held throughout the country. Denis Hayes, the national organizer of Earth Day 1970, later called it "the largest organized demonstration in human history."[27] It certainly showed that the number of Americans embracing environmentalism was large and growing.

ORGANIZING EARTH DAY

For such an enormous event, Earth Day had fairly modest beginnings. It was first conceived by Gaylord Nelson, a Democratic senator from Wisconsin, in late 1969. At the time, he was one of just a handful of members of Congress who identified themselves as environmentalists. He was deeply disturbed by a number of recent environmental disasters, including a catastrophic oil spill in the Santa Barbara Channel that had occurred earlier in the year.

To increase awareness of environmental issues, Nelson decided to organize a national "teach-in." The term *teach-in* was then used by activists who opposed the American involvement in the Vietnam War (1960–1975) for protests designed to teach others about their cause. Funding the effort with small donations and his speaking fees, Nelson hired a staff of students headed by Hayes, who was then attending Harvard Law School.

From the start, the organizers focused on secondary schools and colleges, on the assumption that students would be the most receptive audience for their message. They chose the date April 22 because it fell between college students' spring break and semester exams. Some opponents to environmentalism, however, claimed that the date was meant to commemorate the birthday of Soviet leader Vladimir Lenin. They maintained that Earth Day was an anti-American plot to spread Communism throughout the United States.

TIME FOR CHANGE

Despite such criticism, interest in Earth Day spread far and wide, much faster than Nelson or anyone else could have imagined. It became clear that, upset by recent environmental problems, more Americans than ever were ready to speak out. In addition to the Santa Barbara oil spill, the news was

On April 22, 1970, environmental activist Denis Hayes organized the first Earth Day to promote awareness and appreciation of Earth's environment. Hayes is pictured here at Environment Teach-In, Inc., headquarters in Washington, D.C., on the first Earth Day.

full of stories about chemically contaminated lakes and waterways, cities engulfed in smog, and sewage washing up on public beaches. One of the most disturbing stories told of a massive fire on the Cuyahoga River near Cleveland, Ohio, a river so clogged with industrial waste that *Time* magazine said, "It oozes rather than flows."[28] The idea of river water catching on fire convinced many readers that environmental desecration was out of control.

Earth Day also caught on because many Americans, especially young people, saw it as a natural extension of other expanding social and political movements. During the 1960s, people had taken to the streets to protest the Vietnam War and to demand equal rights for women and African Americans. Protest marches and demonstrations had already proven to be an effective means to publicize and promote these issues, so they seemed natural tools for citizens angered over environmental issues.

Some Americans, fearing change and nervous about the country's future, were uneasy about the antiwar and civil rights movements. The environmental movement seemed far less threatening because most people supported the goal of cleaning up polluted air and water. In fact, many Americans had moved from cities to suburbs so their families could live in a cleaner environment. Not surprisingly, many suburban parents encouraged their children to become involved in environmentalism. Even those wary of other social movements generally supported Earth Day programs in schools and colleges because they believed the events were a safe and worthy outlet for their children's energy.

AFTER EARTH DAY

The mainstream environmental organizations showed far less enthusiasm for the Earth Day festivities. They had virtually nothing to do with its planning and were somewhat stunned by how strongly it was embraced by the public. As Michael McCloskey, then executive director of the Sierra

Club, later recalled: "We were taken aback by the speed or suddenness with which the new forces exploded."[29]

The memberships of these older groups also exploded. During the 1970s, the Sierra Club's membership almost doubled, and the Audubon Society's more than tripled. In the years between 1970 and 1985, the total number of Americans who belonged to environmental groups ballooned from about 500,000 to 2.5 million.

Even as their memberships swelled and their fund-raising soared, the traditional groups struggled to keep up with the times. In the past, they had tended to focus on single issues, usually associated with wilderness and wildlife protection. Now the public was interested in a far broader array of issues. The older groups were also beholden to corporations, which were frequently represented on their boards of directors. The public at this point was identifying these organizations' corporate allies as their enemies in campaigns against pollution and waste.

Some organizations tried to refocus their attention and priorities to appeal to younger environmentalists. The National Wildlife Federation, for instance, created its Cool It! campaign to appeal to young people interested in recycling. Many newcomers to the environmental movement, however, remained skeptical of the traditional groups. (According to Hayes, such activists often dismissed them as "the birds and squirrels people."[30]) Instead, they established their own organizations committed to new problems and concerns.

NEW ORGANIZATIONS

By the end of the 1970s, the number of environmental groups rose from a few hundred to about 3,000. Some were national groups that soon had memberships rivaling those of the much more established organizations. Others were

DAVID BROWER: SHAPING THE AMERICAN ENVIRONMENTAL MOVEMENT

Known for his uncompromising passion and stubborn determination, David Brower (1912–2000) was a major force in the environmental movement for more than 50 years. Growing up in California, he fell in love with the Sierra Mountains during family camping trips. In 1933, Brower joined the Sierra Club and began to participate in the hiking and mountain-climbing outings they sponsored. He eventually guided thousands of others through wilderness areas while he worked with the Sierra Club's program. An accomplished rock climber, Brower, in 1939, became the first person to climb to the top of Shiprock, a famed rock formation in New Mexico.

When the United States entered World War II, Brower enlisted in the army. He served with the 10th Mountain Division of the U.S. Army, training soldiers to scale mountain cliffs in Europe. After the war, he returned to California, where he worked as an editor at the University of California Press.

In 1952, Brower became the executive director of the Sierra Club. During his 17-year tenure, the organization grew enormously, enlarging its membership from 2,000 to 77,000. Drawing on his background in publishing, Brower increased public awareness of environmental issues through a series of Sierra Club books and publications. While at the Sierra Club, Brower spearheaded successful campaigns

tiny, sometimes made up of just a few neighbors who held meetings around a kitchen table.

One of the major new organizations that grew out of Earth Day was Environmental Action. Founded in 1970, it aggressively sought legislation to clean up toxic waste and reform the nation's energy policy. Other new organizations were less concerned with lobbying Washington lawmakers. They instead wanted to organize citizens to take direct action on environmental issues. These included Friends to stop the constructions of dams at Dinosaur National Monument and the Grand Canyon.

Due to disagreements with the board of directors, Brower resigned from the Sierra Club in 1969 and founded Friends of the Earth, which dealt with international environmental issues. After leaving the organization in 1986, he devoted much of his time to the Earth Island Institute, which he established in 1982. Working with these groups, Brower played an important role in the creation of several national parks and national seashores and in the preservation of forest lands in the West. His life and work were celebrated in the PBS television program *For Earth's Sake* (1990) and the documentary feature *Monumental: David Brower's Fight for Wild America* (2004).

On November 5, 2000, David Brower died of cancer at the age of 88. The *San Francisco Chronicle* took the occasion to honor his legacy: "His career spanned an era when the public began to question human effects on the environment. Dams, nuclear power plants and the private use of federal lands were accepted ideas until Brower and other environmental leaders vigorously doubted the concepts. For this, he is owed thanks."*

---

* "Editorial: The Legacy of David Brower," *San Francisco Chronicle* (November 8, 2000).

of the Earth, established in 1969 by former Sierra Club head David Brower. After wrangling with the Sierra Club board over financial issues, Brower announced that his new organization would take a different approach. He said it would pursue "a greater emphasis on international issues, a more direct ideological role through an expanded publishing effort, and a more expansive agenda, including but not limited to traditional wilderness and resources policy themes."[31]

Perhaps the most noteworthy environmental group to emerge in the early 1970s was Greenpeace. It began with a protest initiated by three men from Vancouver, Canada. They were former employees of the Sierra Club, who quit because the organization refused to speak out against nuclear testing. On September 15, 1971, they and nine others set out in a boat and sailed toward Amchitka Island off the coast of Alaska to take their own stand. There, they hoped to stop an underground nuclear bomb test by the U.S. government. Because of bad weather, their boat had to turn back. The publicity surrounding the event was enough, however, to persuade the government to abandon its testing plans.

Attracted by the willingness of these activists to risk their lives for their convictions, several organizations calling themselves Greenpeace grew up. (In 1979, they came together to form Greenpeace International, with its base of operations in Amsterdam.) Throughout the 1970s, Greenpeace members became known for their commitment to social justice and their passionate concern for the planet. In addition to nuclear testing, they took on other popular issues, which included saving endangered whales, sea lions, and other ocean animals.

ENVIRONMENTALISM IN POPULAR CULTURE

In 1979, the film *The China Syndrome* was released in American theaters. The thriller told the story of a reporter who discovers dangerous safety breaches at a nuclear power plant outside Los Angeles. For years, opposition to nuclear power had been emerging as an important environmental issue, so the movie was meant to capitalize on this topical subject. To the nuclear power industry, though, the film constituted a threat. The industry launched a full-scale attack on the film and the accuracy of its presentation of nuclear power safety issues.

Twelve days after the film's release, however, an event signaled that the movie was not so far off the mark. On March 28, 1979, the Three Mile Island nuclear power plant near Harrisburg, Pennsylvania, experienced a cooling-system valve failure, creating the worst commercial power plant accident in the history of the United States. The event eerily mirrored an accident portrayed in *The China Syndrome.* The news of the Three Mile Island accident, along with publicity surrounding the film, helped draw more attention to nuclear power safety than ever before.

Nuclear power has long been a controversial form of energy because of its potential threat to the environment. On March 28, 1979, the Three Mile Island nuclear power plant, just south of Harrisburg, Pennsylvania, experienced a partial meltdown in one of its generators. Although no one died in the incident, the cleanup lasted 14 years and cost nearly $1 billion.

Though particularly notable, *The China Syndrome* was only one example of how environmentalism crept into popular culture during the 1970s. Numerous popular songs—including Marvin Gaye's "Mercy, Mercy Me" and Joni Mitchell's "Big Yellow Taxi"—contained lyrics about environmental concerns, whereas writers such as Edward Abbey (*The Monkey Wrench Gang*) and Dr. Seuss (*The Lorax*) used fiction to share their own stances on these issues. Possibly from a more cynical perspective, writers and producers in television and film recognized that environmentalism was a sellable product. Even Saturday morning cartoons were filled with environmental messages. In one example, *Yogi's Gang* depicted a team of cartoon animals taking on villains that included Mr. Pollution and Mr. Smog.

TAKING ACTION

Perhaps the most memorable environmental image from the 1970s came from an extremely popular televised public service announcement for the Keep America Beautiful campaign. First airing on the second Earth Day celebration in 1971, the spot showed an American Indian man paddling a canoe through a polluted river to a bank covered with garbage. When he emerged from the boat, a passing motorist threw trash out of the car, which landed at the Indian's feet. The final image was a close-up view of this man's face, where a single teardrop fell down his cheek as an unseen narrator said, "People start pollution, people can stop it."

It was a message that Americans took to heart in the 1970s. Many people who did not attend protests or join environmental groups still allowed new ideas about the environment to change their beliefs and behaviors. A few completely altered the way they lived. Often part of the hippie youth movement, they turned their back on traditional

American society and moved to rural communes to live off the land. (The most successful commune, The Farm, located in Tennessee, still exists.)

For most Americans, however, the lifestyle changes they made were far less drastic. People concerned about trash began to buy products with less excess packaging or to take their bottles and newspapers to a recycling center. People disturbed by litter organized cleanups of public parks and roadside areas. People upset by humans' use of animals for food became vegetarians. People alarmed by pesticides in the food supply planted their own organic gardens. Although on an individual level these changes may have seemed small, they signaled something much bigger: Environmentalism had become a permanent part of everyday American life.

Legislating Change

66 **T**he great question of the seventies is, shall we surrender to our surroundings, or shall we make our peace with nature and begin to make reparations for the damage we have done to our air, to our land, and to our water? . . . Clean air, clean water, open spaces—these should once again be the birthright of every American. If we act now, they can be."[32]

In February 1970, U.S. Republican president Richard M. Nixon said these words to the nation in his State of the Union address. Nearly half of the speech, in fact, was devoted to environmental policy. Nixon wanted to make it clear that improvement of the environment was at the top of his agenda.

Environmental issues were not a personal concern of Nixon's, however. His interest was largely political. When he first became president, Nixon was taken by surprise at the popularity of environmentalism. As Undersecretary of the Interior John C. Whitaker explained, "We were totally unprepared for the tidal wave of public opinion in favor of cleaning up the environment that was about to engulf us."[33]

Quickly, though, Nixon discovered that he could increase his popularity with voters if he championed new environmental policies. After Earth Day, this message was even clearer. The public had spoken, and every politician could see that it was now far easier to support environmental legislation than to oppose it.

CREATING THE EPA

The first major environmental law passed during the Nixon administration was the National Environment Policy Act (NEPA), which was signed into law on live television on January 1, 1970. The law placed restrictions on all major projects initiated by the federal government that could have a significant impact on the environment, which included most building projects, such as construction of bridges or roads.

Before such projects could begin, the government was required first to prepare an environmental impact statement (also known as an EIS). This document was to detail how the project would affect the environment and outline any possible alternatives to the project. Even before construction started, the public would now know if a major federal project was likely to cause environmental damage, giving concerned citizens the chance to fight it.

Even more importantly, the NEPA created a brand-new federal agency—the Environmental Protection Agency, or EPA. The EPA was to administer all the federal government's existing and future programs concerning the environment. The EPA started out with a staff of 6,000 and an annual budget of $455 million. By the end of the 1970s, it had 13,000 employees and an annual budget of $1.6 billion. In just one decade, the EPA ballooned into one of the largest agencies in the U.S. government.

LANDMARK LEGISLATION

Once the EPA was created, the pressure was on. With Nixon's support, Congress passed bill after bill, addressing a host of

In 1969, Congress passed the National Environment Policy Act (NEPA), which was signed into law by President Richard Nixon on January 1, 1970. The law requires all federal agencies to determine the environmental impact of programs they fund.

long-ignored environmental problems. In a few years, it enacted more than a dozen major pieces of legislation, paying particular attention to laws aimed at reducing air and water pollution. These acts included such landmark legislation as the following:

★ *The Clean Air Act Extension of 1970.* A major revision of the Clean Air Act of 1963, the law set regulations for air quality, established new limits for auto emissions, and required that the EPA enforce these regulations.

★ *The Federal Environmental Pesticide Control Act of 1972.* This act created a system for regulating pesticide use in the United States.

★ *The Safe Drinking Water Act of 1974.* This law allowed the EPA to set standards for the quality of drinking water provided by all public water systems.

★ *The Toxic Substances Control Act of 1976.* This act called for the regulation of new chemicals and the determination of any health and environmental dangers they posed.

Another milestone in environmental legislation was the Endangered Species Act of 1973, which gave the U.S. Fish and Wildlife Service the authority to determine which species were in danger of extinction and to take whatever measures were necessary to protect them. The language of the act was unusually blunt. It laid blame for endangered species on "economic growth and development untempered by adequate concern and conservation"[34] and stated that these species had an "esthetic, ecological, educational, historical, recreational, and scientific value to the Nation and its people."[35]

PART OF THE SYSTEM

Not everyone was satisfied with this flurry of legislation. For instance, some people wanted laws that would eliminate pollutants altogether, rather than merely adopting limits on their use. Nevertheless, the new laws represented a major victory for environmentalists, especially those who worked for large national environmental groups. In many cases, representatives of organizations such as the Sierra Club and the Audubon Society played an important role in drafting the actual legislation.

As membership in these organizations grew in the 1970s, so did their staffs. They hired lawyers, scientists, publicists, fund-raisers, and, perhaps most importantly, lobbyists, who were charged with meeting with lawmakers and persuading them to support environmental causes. By the end of the decade, professional environmentalists had become a permanent fixture in Washington, D.C. They often moved back and forth from jobs at the EPA to jobs in environmental organizations. Some activists were critical of the situation. They sniped that these professional environmentalists should be fighting, not joining, the Washington, D.C., establishment.

INTERNATIONAL INTEREST

As the American environmental movement grew, people and politicians in other nations began to take notice, as well. Because of this interest, the United Nations sponsored an international environmental conference in Stockholm, Sweden, in 1972. Officially called the United Nations Conference on the Human Environment, it was best known as the Stockholm Conference. Representatives from 113 nations and from approximately 400 organizations attended.

At the conference, the attendees declared that there was "an urgent desire of the peoples of the whole world" to "bring about the protection and improvement of the human environment."[36] They also established the United Nations Environment Programme, an organization that coordinates all of the United Nations' projects and policies relating to the environment. Most importantly, the conference marked the beginning of an international effort to solve environmental

In 1972, the United Nations sponsored the Conference on the Human Environment, or Stockholm Conference, which was attended by representatives from 113 nations, including Shirley Temple Black, the U.S. representative. The conference was held to discuss global environmental problems.

problems affecting many nations. At the same time, however, it also underscored the difficulties of getting nations to work together. For example, at the Stockholm Conference, it was clear that the priorities of poor nations, which resisted any policies that might harm their economies, were not always the same as those of wealthy, industrialized countries such as the United States.

New global awareness of the environment also gave birth to new political parties. The first "green parties"—that is, political parties focused on environmental issues—grew up in Australia and New Zealand in 1972. The next year, the Ecology Party was established in England. By the end of the 1970s, at least a dozen countries, mostly in Europe, had active green parties. Although they did not win many elections, they did bring attention to environmental issues. Often, when established parties realized certain environmental policies were popular with the public, they would begin to support them, too.

THE MOVEMENT FLOUNDERS

The United States did not have its own green party until the 1980s, possibly because in the 1970s its government was already focused on the creation of environmental policy. By the end of the decade, however, Washington's enthusiasm for environmentalism had begun to fade somewhat.

When Nixon resigned from office in 1974, Vice President Gerald Ford was sworn in as the new president. Ford's support for environmentalism was lukewarm. He was far more interested in economic policy, understandably since America was suffering a serious recession. The economic downturn was caused in large part by a spike in oil and gasoline prices in 1973. As Ford explained his priorities, "I pursue the goal of clean air and pure water, but I must also pursue the objective of maximum jobs and continued economic progress. Unemployment is as real and sickening a blight as any pollutant that threatens the nation."[37]

LOIS GIBBS: GRASSROOTS ORGANIZER OF THE LOVE CANAL HOMEOWNERS ASSOCIATION

When Lois Gibbs was 21 years old, she and her husband bought a house in the Love Canal community outside Buffalo, New York. A stay-at-home mother with a high school education who was raising two young children in the suburbs, she seemed an unlikely activist. Since 1978, however, when Gibbs learned Love Canal was built on a toxic waste dump, she has become one of the most successful grassroots organizers in the American environmental movement.

Gibbs got involved in the toxic waste issue when her son became sick with epilepsy. Many of her neighbors were also ill with relatively rare ailments. Organizing the Love Canal Homeowners Association, Gibbs tried to get help from the state and federal government, but they tried to downplay the health risks posed by the toxins. While she struggled to get officials to take the problem seriously, the Love Canal families were in an incredible bind: The longer they stayed in their homes, the sicker they were likely to become, but they could not afford to leave because no one would buy their houses.

Finally, Gibbs had had enough. To get media attention, she and some supporters took two officials from the Environmental Protection Agency (EPA) hostage. Surrounded by armed FBI agents, Gibbs released the hostages on live national television. The EPA soon gave in and agreed to fund the evacuation of Love Canal residents. Gibbs, however, was not satisfied. She wanted the government to give her and her neighbors the purchase price of their homes. Gibbs made her case on a national talk show and blamed President Jimmy Carter for not taking action. Unnerved by this negative publicity in the middle of his difficult reelection campaign, Carter eventually agreed to Gibbs's demands. Gibbs's activism was also the driving force behind the creation of the EPA's Superfund, a pool of money devoted to finding and cleaning up toxic sites.

After evacuating Love Canal, Gibbs moved to Washington, D.C., where she established the Citizens'

(continued on page 66)

(continued from page 65)

Clearinghouse for Hazardous Waste (later renamed the Center for Health, Environment and Justice, or CHEJ) in 1981. The organization offered support and training to grassroots groups fighting toxic waste problems in their communities. The only national environmental organization headed by the leader of a grassroots movement, the CHEJ has helped more than 10,000 groups since it was founded.

As executive director of CHEJ, Gibbs travels across the United States, lecturing about the dangers of toxic chemicals, especially to children. She has also written several books, including *Love Canal: My Story* (1982) and *Dying from Dioxin: A Citizen's Guide to Reclaiming Our Health and Rebuilding Democracy* (1995). In 1982, CBS aired a made-for-television movie about her life, titled *Lois Gibbs: The Love Canal Story.* Gibbs has received numerous honors for her work, including the Goldman Environmental Prize and honorary degrees from the State University of New York and Haverford College. In 2003, she was nominated for the Nobel Peace Prize.

Ford's successor, Jimmy Carter, the former Democratic governor of Georgia, was far friendlier to Washington environmentalists. President Carter welcomed them to the White House and encouraged their input. In a belated effort to deal with the oil crisis, Carter also tried to develop programs to limit oil and gas consumption. In 1977, he persuaded Congress to establish the Department of Energy, which was to administer energy policy and nuclear safety. The new department set voluntary recommendations for conserving energy. Carter himself made a show of living by these guidelines. He turned down the thermostat in the White House to conserve energy and mandated that the presidential residence would go without Christmas lights to save electricity. However, the American people showed little enthusiasm for voluntary conservation efforts, especially as their anger grew over high oil prices, inflation, and other economic woes.

In its final days, the Carter administration did succeed in passing one last important piece of environmental legislation—the Comprehensive Environmental Response, Compensation, and Liability Act of 1980, also known as the Superfund law. The act levied a tax on chemical and petroleum companies to help fund toxic waste cleanups. It also allocated $1.6 billion to this Superfund, to be spent over the next five years.

As the 1970s came to an end, despite some setbacks, the environmental movement was still going strong. Thousands of environmental groups of all sizes were organizing newcomers to the movement. The EPA, armed with a host of new environmental laws, was policing industrial polluters more effectively than ever before. In addition, a large swath of the public still gave its firm support to environmental causes. One poll in 1980 found that 55 percent of Americans declared they were sympathetic to the goals of environmentalists.

In 10 years, the environmental movement had grown bigger and stronger. However, as the next decade began, its leaders would find themselves facing new and difficult challenges. Not everyone was pleased with the sprawling movement, including some powerful enemies ready and willing to do whatever they could to stop it.

7

The 1980s Backlash

Defeating Jimmy Carter's reelection bid, Republican Ronald Reagan was elected president in November 1980. During his inauguration speech, Reagan, referring to the nation's economic troubles, announced that "government is not the solution to our problems: government is the problem."[38] In Reagan's mind, Americans needed to "get government off our backs" and "set business free again."[39]

For environmentalists, Reagan's words were disturbing. Throughout the 1970s, they had worked hard to assemble a system of regulations on business and industry to deal with a host of problems—from pollution to pesticides to toxic waste. Now it was clear, however, that the new administration was determined to dismantle as many environmental safeguards as it could. For Reagan and his probusiness supporters, environmental regulation, like government in general, was a problem—one they wanted to get rid of once and for all.

Business leaders and conservative politicians cheered Reagan's campaign against environmentalism. Many voters did, as well. Weary of hearing doomsday scenarios, they had soured on environmentalism. They were tired, too, of years of social and cultural upheaval associated with the civil rights, antiwar, and women's movements. To them, Reagan's upbeat message was a comfort. Even though the country was mired in an economic recession, Reagan assured his followers that

America remained a great nation and that everyone would prosper, just as long as industry could conduct business unhampered by needless rules and regulations.

GORSUCH'S EPA

When Carter was president, he had solar panels installed on the roof of the White House to show his commitment to energy conservation. In his first days in office, Reagan made a symbolic gesture of his own: He ordered that the panels be ripped down. With this simple action, Reagan showed his complete contempt for his predecessor's environmental policies.

An even more important demonstration was his appointment of Anne Gorsuch as the administrator of the EPA. A corporate lawyer from Colorado, Gorsuch had worked for the mining and agricultural industries and had helped companies oppose the EPA's regulations. From the beginning of her tenure, Gorsuch wanted to undermine the agency. For many posts, she appointed people who, like her, had worked for corporations that sought to evade environmental laws. Gorsuch also oversaw the slashing of the EPA's budget by about $200 million. Its staff was cut by about 23 percent.

Not surprisingly, no major environmental legislation was passed while Gorsuch was at the EPA. In addition, the gutting of the agency's budget sent a clear message to the oil, automobile, mining, and timber industries. Its teeth gone, the EPA could do little to enforce existing environmental regulations, freeing these industries simply to ignore them.

MIRED IN SCANDAL

Environmentalists were furious over Gorsuch's appointment, but they were appalled by Reagan's choice for the secretary of the Department of the Interior—James Watt. Watt was a founder of the Mountain State Legal Foundation, a law firm that used contributions from corporations to challenge environmental regulations and to eliminate restrictions on the commercial use of public lands. As head of the

In January 1981, President Ronald Reagan appointed James Watt secretary of the Interior. The selection was controversial because Watt was the founder of Mountain State Legal Foundation, a law firm that opposed restrictions on the commercial use of public lands.

Department of the Interior, Watt sought to lease shorelands and wilderness areas to oil and gas companies and hurry the sale of public lands to private firms, often at prices well below the market value.

Watt's actions drew criticism from many members of Congress, Democrats and Republicans alike. He was also attacked by the Sierra Club and other environmental groups. In October 1981, they presented Congress with a "Dump Watt" petition, calling for Watt's dismissal. The petition had more than one million signatures.

Two years later, the Senate finally pressured Watt to resign, not because of his environmental policies, but because of an offensive remark. (He commented that a Senate advisory panel consisted of "a black, a woman, two Jews and a cripple."[40]) Watt was further discredited when, in 1996, he pleaded guilty to withholding documents during a grand jury investigation that involved his dealings as a lobbyist in the late 1980s.

Gorsuch's tenure at the EPA also ended in scandal. In 1983, the House of Representatives began to investigate the mismanagement of more than one billion dollars earmarked for the Superfund toxic waste cleanup program. She and 20 other top EPA employees refused to testify and were found in contempt of Congress. Gorsuch resigned from her post and later complained that the Reagan administration had not provided her with adequate legal support.

To stem the crisis at the EPA, Reagan appointed William D. Ruckelshaus, the first head of the EPA under Nixon, to become the agency's temporary administrator. Ruckelshaus later recalled, "The agency was in such a state of turmoil that the main thing that needed to be done was to calm it down and put it back to work."[41] Ruckelshaus worked to rebuild the agency and to renew the public's trust in its value and achievements.

After Reagan's reelection in 1984, Lee M. Thomas was brought in to take over the agency. Reagan's second term saw no major new environmental acts, but environmentalists did see some victories in the strengthening of a few existing laws, including the Safe Drinking Water Act and the Superfund legislation.

GROWING STRONGER

For environmentalists, the Reagan era was a nightmare in many ways. In the 1970s, they had become accustomed to success, as, year after year, new laws designed to address environmental problems had come into existence. In the 1980s, however, all that forward momentum came to an end. At best, environmentalists believed they were treading water, and, at worst, they feared losing the gains they had fought so hard for in the previous decade.

In one way, though, the Reagan presidency was a boon to environmentalism. Reagan's policies frightened many Americans who were sympathetic to environmental causes but had not bothered to get involved in the movement. For the first time, many felt compelled to take action. As a result, membership in the major environmental groups again shot up. By 1990, the 10 largest groups had 7.2 million members. Only half-jokingly, one environmental lobbyist quipped that he was sorry to see James Watt resign because "he was the best organizer we ever had."[42]

Some American environmentalists, however, thought that these groups were not doing enough to fight Reagan's environmental policies. They complained that the major environmental groups were working too closely with hostile lawmakers and were too willing to compromise to make even the slightest gain. Critics charged that professional environmentalists had lost the vision and passion they had in the movement's early years.

These frustrations gave birth to two trends within the movement: the rise of grassroots activism and the emergence of radical environmentalism. Although grassroots and radical groups used different tactics, both tended to focus on specific local problems often ignored by both the EPA and the big environmental groups.

GRASSROOTS ACTION

Grassroots groups generally arose quickly and spontaneously as neighbors became concerned about an environmental threat to their community. For instance, grassroots activists might come together to keep a nuclear power plant from being built in their town, to reduce pollutants emitted by a local factory, or to insist on the cleanup of an industrial waste dump close to their homes.

Grassroots groups were often made up of people who had never been involved in politics before. Nevertheless, many groups proved remarkably effective, probably because, for them, the fight was so personal. With the health of their families, friends, and neighborhood on the line, grassroots activists were reluctant to compromise and refused to give up. Generally, they waged their battles with conventional tools, such as organizing letter-writing campaigns, canvassing door to door, staging protest demonstrations, and initiating lawsuits. Sometimes, otherwise law-abiding activists committed acts of civil disobedience—that is, they purposely broke a law they believed was unjust—to demonstrate complete commitment to their cause.

Unlike the membership of the older environmental groups, that of grassroots organizations was fairly diverse. The major environmental groups were generally led by affluent white men. In contrast, grassroots groups were often composed of middle-class and working-class neighbors and frequently had women and members of minority groups in leadership roles.

RADICAL ACTS

Like grassroots organizers, radical environmentalists believed that their voices were not being heard by the government or by professional environmentalists. Many, in fact, had at one time worked for major environmental groups but had become disillusioned. They concluded that the big groups' emphasis on working within the system was unproductive. Radical activists wanted to do far more than making sure laws were passed. They thought that, to save the planet, industrialized America had to remake its economy and society completely.

The radical groups also believed that they could bring about meaningful change only by being aggressive in their words and actions. They also believed that their goals were important enough to justify illegal acts of vandalism and violence. These actions became known as ecosabotage or ecotage. (More recently, opponents have dubbed them ecoterrorism.)

One of the most radical environmental groups to spring up was Earth First! It was established in the spring of 1980 by Dave Foreman and other longtime environmentalists who were fed up with working for traditional organizations. They believed in direct action against companies and institutions that were harming the environment. For example, Earth Firsters damaged bulldozers on public lands, cut down billboards, pulled up survey stakes, and drove spikes into trees to discourage their destruction by chainsaws. In the mid-1980s, they began to engage in "tree-sits," during which activists sat in trees that timber companies wanted to cut down.

ENVIRONMENTAL PHILOSOPHIES

The Earth First! activists drew on the work of Norwegian philosopher Arne Naess. Naess rejected the notion that the needs of humans should dictate their relationship

In 1980, environmental activist Dave Foreman established Earth First!
The organization practices a policy of "No Compromise in Defense
of Mother Earth!" but has recently become more volatile and some
critics have labeled it an ecoterrorist group. Here, two members of
Earth First! hold a banner in front of the Lincoln Memorial that says,
"Equal rights for all species. Save the rainforest."

with nature, an idea he considered shallow. Instead, Naess
advocated what he called deep ecology. This theory held that
all living organisms had an equal claim to the natural world
and dismissed the notion that humanity was inherently more
valuable than other forms of life.

Another ecological philosophy that gained popularity
in the 1980s was ecofeminism. This belief brought together
ideas from the environmental movement and the women's
movement of the 1970s. It saw a common thread between
men's domination over women and humankind's domination
over nature. Accordingly, ecofeminists had twin goals in
their challenge of the American social system that placed

THE MONKEY WRENCH GANG

Since its first publication in 1975, *The Monkey Wrench Gang* by novelist Edward Abbey has become a cult classic. It tells the story of a group of profane misfits who band together to battle their mutual enemies—anyone whose actions threaten to destroy the natural beauty of the American Southwest. Abbey's novel is said to have been a direct influence on the radical environmental group Earth First! which often used ecosabotage as a tactic.

In this excerpt, three members of the gang—Smith, Hayduke, and Sarvis (the doctor)—discuss how they can strike back against Utah's Glen Canyon Dam, a symbol of destructive development:

> "You know what we ought to do," the doctor said. "We ought to blow [up] that dam . . ." [A bit of Hayduke's foul tongue had loosened his own.]
> "How?" said Hayduke.
> "That ain't legal," Smith said.
> "You prayed for an earthquake, you said."
> "Yeah, but there ain't no law agin that."
> "You were praying with malicious intent."
> "That's true. I pray that way all the time."
> "Bent on mischief and the destruction of government property."
> "That's right, Doc."
> "That's a felony."
> > "It ain't just a misdemeanor?"
> > "It's a felony."
> > "How?" said Hayduke.
> > "How what?"
> > "How do we blow up the dam?"
> > "Which dam?"

men above women—to end the exploitation of women and to stop the degradation of the planet.

Environmentalists of the 1980s also embraced the Gaia hypothesis. First developed in 1969 by British chemist James

"Any dam."

"Now you're talking," Smith said. "But Glen Canyon Dam first. I claim that one first."

"I hate that dam," Smith said. "That dam flooded the most beautiful canyon in the world."

"We know," Hayduke said. "We feel the same way you do. But let's think about easier things first. I'd like to knock down some of them power lines they're stringing across the desert. And those new tin bridges up by Kite. And the . . . road-building they're doing all over the canyon country. We could put in a good year just taking the . . . bulldozers apart."

"Hear, hear," the doctor said. "And don't forget the billboards. And the strip mines. And the pipelines. And the new railroad from Black Mesa to Page. And the coal-burning power plants. And the copper smelters. And the uranium mines. And the nuclear power plants. And the computer centers. And the land and cattle companies. And the wildlife poisoners. And the people who throw beer cans along the highways."

"I throw beer cans along the . . . highways," Hayduke said. "Why . . . shouldn't I throw . . . beer cans along the . . . highways?"

"Now, now. Don't be so defensive."

"Hell," Smith said, "I do it too. Any road I wasn't consulted about that I don't like, I litter. It's my religion."

"Well now," the doctor said. "I hadn't thought about that. Stockpile the stuff along the highways. Throw it out the window. Well . . . why not?"

"Doc," said Hayduke, "it's liberation."*

* Edward Abbey, *The Monkey Wrench Gang* (Philadelphia: Lippincott, 1975).

Lovelock, it held that the Earth and all life on it work together as a self-regulating system. The hypothesis, named after the Greek goddess of the Earth, was controversial among scientists but was embraced by the public. Many people were comforted by the idea that the planet functioned much like an organism, naturally constructed to sustain its own life.

Another concept that emerged in the 1980s was that of environmental racism, which dealt with the tendency of the government and even environmentalists to ignore environmental problems that affected minority populations. For instance, urban communities of African Americans and Hispanics were often plagued by pollution, and the reservation lands of American Indians were frequently used as toxic and nuclear waste dumps. To address these inequities, the environmental justice movement sprang up. Its beginnings are sometimes traced to a 1985 protest in Warren County, North Carolina, where about 500 protestors gathered to denounce a chemical landfill planned for this rural area with a largely African-American population. Since then, many similar grassroots efforts have emerged to protect minority communities from environmental threats.

In the 1970s, the environmental movement seemed like a train, barreling farther and faster as each year passed. In the 1980s, the Reagan administration did its best to stop this momentum. Nevertheless, the environmental movement continued to grow as it embraced new activists, new tactics, and new ideas. The train may have slowed down, but it was still moving forward.

8

Losing Influence

In its first issue of 1989, *Time* magazine's cover story highlighted the peculiar weather patterns the United States had seen the year before—a three-month drought in the middle of the country that had destroyed much of its grain harvest, a seven-week heat wave that drove temperatures above 100°F (37.8°C), and a dry spell that set off a wave of fires in western forests. The story also noted the huge amount of garbage—from raw sewage to medical waste—that had been washing up on America's beaches. These oddities led the magazine's editorial staff to make an unprecedented decision:

> [T]his year's bout of freakish weather and environmental horror stories seemed to act as a powerful catalyst for worldwide public opinion. Everyone suddenly sensed that this gyrating globe, this precious repository of all the life that we know of, was in danger. No single individual, no event, no movement captured imaginations or dominated headlines more than the clump of rock and soil and water and air that is our common home. Thus in a rare but not unprecedented departure from its tradition of naming a Man of the Year, *Time* has designated Endangered Earth as Planet of the Year for 1988.[43]

ENVIRONMENTAL CANDIDATE

Environmental issues had also played a crucial role in the 1988 presidential election. With polls showing the public's continuing concern over environmental issues, Reagan's vice president, George H. W. Bush, declared himself the "environmental candidate"[44] during the campaign, an unusual maneuver for a Republican. Bush repeatedly slammed his Democratic rival, Michael Dukakis, for ignoring the pollution in Boston Harbor while Dukakis served as governor of Massachusetts. According to some pollsters, Bush's charge energized voters and contributed significantly to his victory.

Once in office, Bush pleased environmentalists by the appointment of William K. Reilly as administrator of the EPA. Reilly had previously been the president of the World Wildlife Fund, an international conservation organization. The appointment suggested a departure from the Reagan era, when antienvironmentalists were commonly placed in important government posts.

Early in President Bush's tenure, the federal government moved to strengthen several environmental laws. Most noteworthy were amendments to the Clean Air Act designed to toughen existing emissions standards and deal with growing concerns over acid rain—precipitation contaminated with sulfur dioxide that was disrupting the chemical balance of soil and water sources. The law addressed the problem through a program of emissions trading (also called cap and trade). This set limits, or caps, on the pollutants a company could release into the air. If a company fell below that limit, it received credits that it could then sell to polluters that had exceeded their limit.

EARTH DAY REVISITED

The same year the Clean Air Act was amended, the United States celebrated the twentieth anniversary of Earth Day. The first Earth Day had been cobbled together quickly, in the end surprising everyone with its size and scope. The anniversary celebration, however, was much more organized.

The traditional environmental groups got on board, working hard to make sure that Earth Day 1990 would be a big event. Gathering more than $3 million from corporate sponsors, the organizers arranged for 3,000 events, including a prime-time Earth Day television special.

More than 25 million Americans participated in Earth Day 1990. This time around, however, the celebration was international, with more than 140 countries involved. Throughout the world, a total of 100 million people took part in Earth Day 1990 festivities.

Unlike the first Earth Day, the anniversary celebration was also a commercial enterprise. Manufacturers of every product imaginable wanted to be associated with the event; they knew it would make their wares more attractive to environmentally conscious consumers. In September 1991, *Time* magazine, reporting on the "new wave of eco-consumerism," explained, "With polls showing that nearly 90% of American consumers are concerned about the environmental impact of what they buy, many companies are spending big sums to develop an earth-hugging image."[45] As the article noted, however, many of the new "green" consumers had only a passing interest in environmentalism. It quoted one as saying, "I'm not real involved in the environmental movement, but this is something I can do to help."[46]

DISAPPOINTING RECORD

Although Earth Day 1990 reinvigorated public support, the environmental movement faltered during the rest of the Bush administration. The president did little to live up to his promises as the "environmental candidate." Formerly a Texas oil executive, Bush repeatedly showed that he was far more interested in helping the oil industry than in furthering the environmental movement.

(continues on page 84)

BARRY COMMONER: ECOSOCIALIST AND ANTINUCLEAR ACTIVIST

First renowned as a scientific researcher, Barry Commoner became an environmentalist from a moral obligation to speak out against technology's effect on the natural world. Raised in New York City, Commoner was fascinated by nature; as a boy, he often spent time in city parks collecting specimens to examine. In 1941, he was awarded a Ph.D. in biology from Harvard University.

During World War II, Commoner served in the Naval Tactical Air Squadron. The U.S. Navy was concerned that U.S. soldiers fighting in the Pacific might contract insect-borne diseases, so it wanted to spray beaches there with the pesticide DDT. Commoner was assigned to develop a device to spray the chemical. Testing it on a New Jersey beach, he found that the DDT he sprayed had killed thousands of fish in the water. The experience forced him to examine how scientific innovations could have unintended consequences, particularly in regard to their effect on the environment.

After the war, Commoner became a well-regarded professor and scientific researcher. During the 1950s, however, he began to take a more political role. He joined other prominent scientists in speaking out about the potential health hazards of radiation released by atomic bomb tests. Commoner's work helped lead to the Nuclear Test Ban Treaty of 1963, which prohibited all aboveground nuclear weapons testing.

With a $4 million grant from the U.S. Public Health Service, Commoner founded the Center for the Biology of Natural Systems (CBNS) in 1966. This research center studies environmental problems, such as pollution and waste reduction, and explores solar energy and other alternatives to oil and gasoline. Throughout the 1960s and 1970s, Commoner also became a well-known lecturer and author. In his first book, *Science and Survival* (1966), he warned about the environmental destruction wreaked by recent technological advances, from the overuse of pesticides and fertilizers to the pollution caused by large, gasoline-guzzling cars. He revisited similar themes in a series of popular books, including *The Closing Circle* (1971) and *The Politics of Energy* (1979).

FIFTY CENTS   FEBRUARY 2, 1970

TIME

Environment: Nixon's New Issue

ECOLOGIST BARRY COMMONER
The Emerging Science of Survival

In 1980, Barry Commoner became the first environmental activist to run for president when he was the Citizens' Party candidate.

In addition to his environmental positions, Commoner spoke out on broader political issues, especially world poverty. He fully entered the political arena in 1980, when
(continues)

(continued)

he ran for president on the Citizens Party ticket. Commoner and his running mate, American Indian activist LaDonna Harris, received more than 200,000 votes.

The following year, Commoner accepted a professorship of earth and environmental science at Queens College of the City University of New York. He remained in this post until 1987, and he continued his work as the director of CBNS until 2000. In 1997, in honor of his eightieth birthday, Commoner's colleagues gathered for a symposium at New York City's Cooper Union to celebrate his many contributions to the environmental movement.

(continued from page 81)

In March 1989, a giant oil tanker named the *Exxon Valdez* hit Bligh Reef off the coast of Prince William Sound in Alaska. Some 11 million gallons of crude oil spilled into the water, killing thousands of birds, otters, salmon, and other sea animals and destroying hundreds of acres of wildlife habitats. Environmentalists were outraged by this horrible ecological disaster. Bush conceded that it was a "major tragedy"[47] but took little action against the oil industry. To the furor of environmental groups, the president continued to push for more offshore oil exploration. As part of his efforts, Bush tried unsuccessfully to open up the Arctic National Wildlife Refuge for oil drilling. This vast Alaskan refuge includes an 8-million-acre protected wilderness area.

Bush also did little to encourage Americans to reduce their dependence on oil. Some environmentalists thus criticized Bush for invading Iraq during the Gulf War (1990–1991). They complained that the war was launched to secure American oil supplies in the Middle East. In the eyes of these war critics, U.S. soldiers were fighting and dying primarily to further the interests of American oil corporations.

SAVING THE SPOTTED OWL

During the Bush era, corporate interests began to strike out against environmentalists more effectively than ever before. The most publicized instance was the spotted owl controversy of the early 1990s. The spotted owl was named an endangered species in 1990, thanks to a vigorous campaign by environmentalists. They wanted not only to save the owl but also to block timber companies from destroying its natural habitat, the old-growth forests of the Pacific Northwest.

The timber industry then launched a well-funded public relations campaign. It spread the idea that saving the spotted owl was going to cost thousands of jobs for loggers and workers in related fields. (In fact, at the time, increased automation in the logging industry was the primary reason that work was difficult to find for loggers.) The campaign was a great success and convinced many people across the country that environmentalists cared little about working-class families struggling to get by.

The early 1990s also saw the rise of the wise-use movement. This movement was initiated by landowners who resisted environmental regulations on how their land could be used. It was also backed by businesses that wanted access to natural resources on public lands. Especially active in the western United States, wise-use groups lobbied for the weakening of environmental laws and attacked environmentalists as radicals who posed a threat not only to the business community but also to American society. Environmental organizations answered strongly, charging that wise-use advocates were just trying to make money at

During the early 1990s, the Spotted Owl created quite a controversy in the Pacific Northwest. Environmentalists wanted to protect the endangered owl's natural habitat and the only way to do that was by preserving the old-growth forests of Oregon and Washington State.

the expense of the environment. In a letter to its members, the Sierra Club issued a blistering warning: "[W]e are confronted by a super-financed, anti-environment juggernaut that is craftily masquerading behind a totally deceitful public relations 'wise use' blitz to conceal their profit-driven designs. . . . They will stop at nothing to destroy us and the entire environmental movement."[48]

COPING WITH GLOBAL THREATS

While dealing with growing antienvironmentalism, environmentalists also were challenged by emerging problems that threatened not only the United States but also the entire Earth. One such problem was the thinning of the ozone layer—the layer of the stratosphere that keeps dangerous ultraviolet light from reaching the Earth's surface. In the 1970s, scientists first proposed that the ozone layer was being depleted and identified the emission of chemical compounds known as chlorofluorocarbons (CFCs) as the cause. By 1989, the United States and most of the world's other nations signed the Montreal Protocol, an international treaty to phase out the production of many ozone-depleting chemicals.

Global warming (also known as climate change) presented another international environmental crisis. In the late 1980s, scientists from the National Aeronautics and Space Administration (NASA) warned that the temperature of the Earth's atmosphere and oceans was rising. The leading cause was the release of carbon dioxide that occurred when fossil fuels (such as gasoline and oil) were burned. This carbon dioxide was holding the sun's radiation close to the Earth's surface, a phenomenon known as the greenhouse effect. Global warming could result in a host of disasters: the flooding of coastal areas; the death of animal and plant species; the spread of epidemic disease; and the disruption of agriculture, leading to famine and war.

In June 1992, the United Nations Environment Programme hosted the Conference on Environment and Development, informally known as the Earth Summit, in Rio de Janeiro, Brazil. Delegations from more than 170 countries gathered there to discuss environmental issues, particularly global warming. Representing the United States, President Bush made his position clear from the start. As he announced at the summit, "To sustain development, we must protect the environment, and to protect the environment, we must sustain development."[49] Citing economic concerns, Bush worked to water down a treaty meant to address global warming, removing all mandatory limits on the emission of gases responsible for the greenhouse effect. Largely because of lack of commitment by the United States to the issues addressed, the Earth Summit failed to achieve much.

THE 1992 ELECTION

Through his performance at the Earth Summit, Bush meant to signal his commitment to American business interests—an important theme of his 1992 reelection campaign. Voters, however, were unimpressed by President Bush's record and instead elected Bill Clinton, formerly the Democratic governor of Arkansas. Environmentalists were pleased by the results. Not only were they glad to see Bush go, but also they were encouraged by Clinton's selection for his vice president—Senator Al Gore of Tennessee. A leader on environmental issues in Congress, Gore was also the author of the book *Earth in the Balance* (1992), in which he stated, "We must make the rescue of the environment the central organizing principle for civilization."[50] Even though Clinton had said little about environmental issues during the campaign, environmentalists assumed he and Gore would make them a priority.

Once again, however, they were disappointed. The Clinton administration was generally supportive of environmentalism, but, in its early years, it was preoccupied with fulfilling the president's campaign promises to improve the economy and develop a plan for universal health care. The White House did make an attempt to push through environmental legislation dealing with a range of issues, including mining regulations on federal lands, air quality,

Environmentalists overwhelmingly supported Democratic candidate and Arkansas governor Bill Clinton in the 1992 presidential election. Clinton is pictured here during a campaign stop in Roland, Arkansas, where he is speaking to members of the Sierra Club. Clinton was only the second presidential candidate to receive the environmental group's endorsement (the first was Theodore Roosevelt).

and unsafe drinking water. Congress, however, rejected all new major laws, except for the California Desert Protection Act of 1994, which preserved millions of acres of wilderness lands in the state.

Matters only grew worse after the midterm elections in November 1994, during which Republicans won a majority of seats in both houses of Congress. Many Republican lawmakers had campaigned with promises to shrink the federal government and loosen its regulation of industry. They were opposed to any new environmental legislation and worked to weaken existing laws. For instance, in 1995, Congress amended the Clean Water Act to lift some pollution restrictions and get rid of requirements for the treatment of contaminated water. It also attempted to slash the budget of the EPA. Vice President Gore angrily spoke out against the cuts: "This is the most insidious part of their agenda—to take away the ability of the EPA and others to enforce environmental laws, by destroying the ability of the government to monitor pollution and to enforce the laws."[51]

THE KYOTO PROTOCOL

In this tense political climate, U.S. representatives headed to Kyoto, Japan, to attend another international conference on climate change. On December 11, 1997, the delegates to the conference reached an agreement called the Kyoto Protocol. It called for 38 industrialized countries to gradually lower their emissions of greenhouse gases. Unlike the global warming agreement negotiated at 1992's Earth Summit, the Kyoto Protocol set mandatory emission limits.

The treaty was ready for signing in March 1998. American supporters of the Kyoto Protocol, however, had a problem. For it to go into effect in the United States, the U.S. Senate had to ratify the treaty—that is, vote to approve it. The Senate, though, had already signaled that it would not ratify the agreement. In July 1997, in a vote of 95 to 0, the Senate had passed a resolution stating that it would accept a mandatory agreement on emissions only if it applied to poorer developing nations, as well as wealthier industrialized ones, which the Kyoto Protocol did not. Vice President Gore signed the protocol in November 1998, but the act was purely symbolic. The Clinton administration did not even try to send it to the Senate for ratification.

By the end of the 1990s, it was clear that many of the worst, most complex environmental problems required global action. In its refusal to ratify the Kyoto Protocol, however, the United States apparently would not be leading the way.

9

Reinventing Environmentalism

66**O**n the issue of the environment, I've never given up. I've never backed down and I never will,"[52] announced Vice President Al Gore when he was nominated for president during the 2000 Democratic National Convention. Gore was the most prominent environmentalist in the United States, but he still thought it was necessary to declare his commitment to the cause. During his time in the White House, he had faced criticism from environmentalists, who believed he had not done enough. The title of a *Time* magazine article from April 1999 summed up many environmentalists' doubts about the candidate: "Is Al Gore a Hero or a Traitor?"[53]

Despite his declaration at the Democratic National Convention, Gore, in fact, had been hesitant to trumpet his environmental record too much during the campaign. He feared that his Republican opponent and the press might use it to brand him a fanatic. Gore remembered how, in 1992, because of his support for the ban on ozone-destroying CFCs, Republican candidate George H. W. Bush took to calling him "ozone man."[54] He also claimed Gore was such an extremist that, if he and Clinton were elected, "we'll be up to our necks in [spotted] owls and out of work for every American."[55] In 2000, his son, the Republican candidate George W. Bush, continued to taunt Gore. On the campaign trail, he joked that Gore "likes electric cars. He just doesn't like making electricity."[56]

Downplaying his environmentalism to avoid ridicule created a problem for Gore: It further angered voters who deeply cared about the environment. Many could not see much difference between Gore and Bush, so they opted to vote for the Green Party candidate, Ralph Nader. Nader received about 2,800,000 votes, at least some of which might have gone to Gore if he had not shied away from a campaign on environmental issues. In the end, Gore lost to the second Bush in one of the closest elections in American history.

THE GEORGE W. BUSH YEARS

Any voter who had thought there was little difference between George W. Bush and Gore on environmental issues soon learned differently. For instance, Bush had pledged during the campaign to require power plants to reduce their emissions of carbon dioxide. Once in office, however, he announced that he had no intention of making good on his promise.

This was just one of many actions taken by the new president that infuriated the environmental community. He refused to support tougher standards for removal of poisonous arsenic from drinking water, banned private lawsuits to add new animals to the endangered species list, and pushed a plan to drill oil in the Arctic National Wildlife Refuge. Bush also appointed Gale Norton as the secretary of the Department of the Interior. Norton had been a powerful player in the antienvironmentalism wise-use movement and a protégé of James Watt, the controversial Interior secretary of the Reagan era.

Most disturbing of all to environmentalists, in 2001, Bush out and out rejected the Kyoto Protocol—the global warming agreement that Gore had signed on behalf of the United

States but that had not yet been ratified by the Senate. The president claimed that he was not convinced global warming was really caused by the burning of fossil fuels by humans. In 2002, Christine Todd Whitman, the administrator of the EPA, issued the *Climate Action Report 2000*, which concluded that global warming is "likely mostly due to human activities."[57] Environmentalists hoped the report would persuade Bush to reconsider his position. Instead, he dismissed the report a few days later by saying it was "put out by the bureaucracy,"[58] which implied it could not be trusted.

Not surprisingly, the environmental legislation championed by the Bush administration was largely designed

The Healthy Forest Act of 2003 was signed into law by President George W. Bush on December 3, 2003. Although the act was purportedly designed to thin forests so that they could not be destroyed by fire, in reality, the law opened up more land for commercial logging.

to loosen regulations. The Healthy Forests Restoration Act of 2003, for instance, was hailed as a means to thin forests in danger of destruction from fire. Major environmental groups, however, opposed the law because it opened more public forest lands to private logging companies.

The response of Bush's EPA to the September 11, 2001 (9/11), terrorist attacks on the World Trade Center and the Pentagon also drew harsh criticism. A week after the attack, Whitman announced that the air and water were safe in the affected areas in New York City. A 2003 report by the inspector general of the EPA, however, said that Whitman's statement was misleading and held that the White House had "convinced [the] EPA to add reassuring statements and delete cautionary ones."[59]

THE DEATH OF ENVIRONMENTALISM?

Although environmentalists loudly denounced the administration's environmental record, the American public seemed to have little interest in the subject. In part, people were distracted by the threat of terrorism and by the U.S. military's wars in Afghanistan and Iraq. To many in the environmental movement, though, the problem seemed broader. The American people said they wanted clean air, clean water, protections for endangered species, and, in general, a healthy planet. Unfortunately, they seemed to have lost their willingness to fight for these things.

Noting the public's apathy, some environmentalists began to place the blame, not on the American people, but on themselves. Among them were public relations consultant Michael Shellenberger and pollster Ted Nordhaus, both of whom had worked for many years for environmental organizations. In 2004, they wrote about their conclusions in an essay with an intentionally provocative title—"The Death of Environmentalism."

Before writing the essay, the authors interviewed 25 leading environmentalists. Although the interviewees agreed the environmental movement seemed stalled, none thought they had to change radically what they were doing. Shellenberger and Nordhaus were disturbed by the response. They argued that the time had come to think of new ways to approach environmental challenges. As they explained, "modern environmentalism, with all of its unexamined assumptions, outdated concepts and exhausted strategies, must die so that something new can live."[60]

The biggest problem of all, Shellenberger and Nordhaus said, was that "the environmental community had still not come up with an inspiring vision, much less a legislative proposal, that a majority of Americans could get excited about."[61] Without being too specific, they explained that the movement needed to craft a message that was inspiring: "Something that would remind people of the American dream: That we are a can-do people capable of achieving great things when we put our mind to it."[62]

The essay set off a firestorm in the environmental community. Many environmentalists were stung by Shellenberger's and Nordhaus's critique and responded strongly with critical essays of their own. Nevertheless, "The Death of Environmentalism" did initiate a heated debate among environmentalists about the most important question facing the movement: What must they do to deal more effectively with the day's worst environmental problems?

GROWING FEARS

The most worrisome threat of all was global warming. In 2003, Europe saw an extreme heat wave, and in 2005, Hurricane Katrina damaged the American city of New Orleans. The weather system is too complex to blame global

THE FUTURE OF THE MOVEMENT

At the October 2004 meeting of the Environmental Grantmakers Association, Michael Shellenberger and Ted Nordhaus presented a paper titled "The Death of Environmentalism." The essay set off a fierce debate and offended many environmentalists. Perhaps its most vocal critic was Carl Pope, the executive director of the nation's oldest environmental group, the Sierra Club: "Before this paper came out, there was a debate going on in the environmental community about how we could more effectively organize ourselves. . . . Shellenberger and Nordhaus have set that debate back, not moved it forward."* Others disagreed, believing many of the points the authors set forth were more than worthy of discussion.

The following excerpt is from the essay's conclusion, a meditation on how the environmental movement should move forward, particularly on the issue of global warming:

> Kevin Phillips recently argued in *Harper's* Magazine that the decline of liberalism began because "liberal intellectuals and policy makers had become too sure of themselves, so lazy and complacent that they failed to pay attention to people who didn't share their opinions."
>
> Environmentalists find themselves in the same place today. We are so certain about what the problem is, and so committed to their legislative solutions, that we behave as though all we need is to tell the literal truth in order to pass our policies.
>
> Environmentalists need to tap into the creative worlds of myth-making, even religion, not to better sell narrow and technical policy proposals but rather to figure out who we are and who we need to be.
>
> Above all else, we need to take a hard look at the institutions the movement has built over the last 30 years. Are

warming specifically for either one of these occurrences, but the extreme weather was consistent with scientists' concerns about what climate change could do.

existing environmental institutions up to the task of imagining the post–global warming world? Or do we now need a set of new institutions founded around a more expansive vision and set of values?

If, for example, environmentalists don't consider the high cost of health care, R&D [research and development] tax credits, and the overall competitiveness of the American auto industry to be "environmental issues," then who will think creatively about a proposal that works for industry, workers, communities and the environment? If framing proposals around narrow technical solutions is an ingrained habit of the environmental movement, then who will craft proposals framed around vision and values?

One thing is certain: If we hope to achieve our objectives around global warming and a myriad of intimately related problems then we need to take an urgent step backwards before we can take two steps forward.

Anyone who has spent time near wide and wild rivers knows that crossing one on stepping stones requires first contemplating the best route. More often than not you must change your route halfway across. But, at the very least, by planning and pursuing a route you become conscious of the choices that you are making, how far you've really come, and where you still must go.

We in the environmental community today find ourselves head-down and knee-deep in the global warming river. It's time we got back to shore and envisioned a new path for the crossing.**

---

* Amanda Griscom Little, "Over Our Dead Bodies: Green Leaders Say Rumors of Environmentalism's Death Are Greatly Exaggerated." Grist, January 13, 2005. Available online at *http://www.grist.org/news/ maindish/2005/01/13/little-responses/#pope*.

** Michael Shellenberger and Ted Nordhaus, "The Death of Environmentalism: Global Warming Politics in a Post-environmental World." Grist, January 13, 2005. Available online at *http://www.grist.org/news/maindish/2005/01/13/doe-reprint*.

Scientists also warned that, in addition to changing weather patterns, the warming of the Earth could melt glaciers and raise sea levels around the world. Because about half of the world's people live near coastlines, rising sea levels could destroy many densely populated areas, including great cities such as Amsterdam, Venice, Cairo, and Shanghai. Poorer people, unable to erect expensive barriers to hold back the rising water, would have to move. Such migrations could set off wars between newcomers and natives, each fighting to control food, drinking water, and dry land areas. A study commissioned by the U.S. Pentagon in 2003 predicted that global warming could produce horrible droughts, mass starvation, and even nuclear war.

Faced with such horrific predictions, many countries, particularly those in Europe, took action. When the Kyoto Protocol went into effect in February 2005, it had been ratified

The Kyoto Protocol, which calls for industrial countries to reduce greenhouse gas emissions, went into effect in February 2005. Every major country in the world, with the exception of the United States and Australia, have signed the agreement. Here, joggers pass a sign in front of the White House urging President George W. Bush to sign the climate change initiative.

by 141 countries (including all industrialized nations except for the United States, Australia, and Monaco). The protocol calls for industrialized countries to reduce greenhouse gases by an average of 5 percent below their 1990 levels by 2012.

DENYING THE PROBLEM

Ironically, the United States, which helped spark the international environmental movement, was doing little to solve the problem of global warming. Why were Americans so hesitant to take on this issue?

The second Bush administration certainly did not make it a priority. President Bush claimed that reduction of greenhouse emissions would destroy the American economy.

In addition to the rejection of the Kyoto Protocol, his administration reduced funding for development of solar and wind power as alternatives to burning fossil fuels. In general, as environmental writer Bill McKibben has stated, the White House's energy plan was "more drilling, more refining, more combusting, more carbon."[63] McKibben added, "It's the policy equivalent of sticking your fingers in your ears and shouting, 'I can't hear you!' over and over again."[64]

Some environmentalists also believed the movement itself was in part to blame. Since its beginnings, the movement has been associated with doomsday scenarios, in which popular writers predicted how an array of environmental problems would lead to the end of the world. When such disasters did not come to pass, the American public naturally began to take predictions of worldwide apocalypse with a grain of salt. Americans, too, have traditionally been an upbeat people and therefore unreceptive to talk of global disaster. As Ted Nordhaus has explained, "We live in an aspirational culture. Gloom and doom narratives don't work. We need to give Americans a vision of the world that is optimistic and hopeful."[65]

There was yet another reason Americans largely ignored the threat of global warming. The energy and automobile industries spent a great deal of money to fund studies intended to confuse the public about the science behind climate change. These studies suggested that some scientific uncertainty about the issue still remained. In fact, however, the great majority of the world's credible scientists agree that global warming is a threat and that it is largely due to human actions.

In January 2007, the nonprofit organization Union of Concerned Scientists issued a report blasting the ExxonMobil Corporation for its role in misleading the American public. The report claimed that ExxonMobil gave $16 million to 43 groups between 1998 and 2005 to produce inaccurate material that questioned the science of global warming. ExxonMobil dismissed the report as "yet another attempt to smear our name and confuse the discussion of the serious issue of CO_2 [carbon dioxide] emissions and global climate change."[66] The following month, as reported in the British newspaper the *Guardian,* the American Enterprise Institute, a lobbying group funded by ExxonMobil, offered a number of scientists and economists $10,000 each in exchange for denouncing a new report released by the Intergovernmental Panel on Climate Change (IPCC) of the United Nations. The report, written by international experts and "widely regarded as the most comprehensive review of climate change science,"[67] concluded that there is no doubt that global warming is real and that human activity is very likely the cause.

NEW COMMITMENT

To challenge those who denied the fact of global warming, former vice president Al Gore appeared in the 2006 feature documentary *An Inconvenient Truth.* The film, based on a multimedia show Gore had presented around the world, discussed the science behind global warming, as well as the economic and political difficulties in attempts to deal with the problem. The movie was greeted with enthusiasm by critics, including *Chicago Sun-Times* reviewer Roger Ebert, who wrote, "You owe it to yourself to see this film. If you do not, and you have grandchildren, you should explain to them why you decided not to."[68] It also performed well at the box office, becoming the third-highest-grossing documentary of all time. Gore has pledged his proceeds to educational campaigns about global warming. Winner of the Academy Award for Best Documentary, the film has also been adopted into the science curricula of many high schools and colleges.

The popularity of *An Inconvenient Truth* suggested that the American public was perhaps now ready to take on this crucial environmental issue. Further evidence of this shift was a flurry of new state and local laws intended to reduce carbon dioxide emissions. The most dramatic advances have occurred in California, where Governor Arnold Schwarzenegger pledged to cut fossil fuel emissions by 30 percent by 2020. The state also passed a law requiring that 20 percent of its electricity come from renewable energy sources, such as solar and wind power, by 2010.

States were also using the courts to push the federal government to follow their lead. For instance, in *Massachusetts v. Environmental Protection Agency*, 12 states, 3 cities, and several environmental groups sued the EPA. They argued that, by the Clean Air Act, the EPA was obligated to regulate auto emissions that contribute to global warning. In April 2007, the Supreme Court found in favor of the plaintiffs. Environmentalists predicted that the decision would encourage more states to take legal action against the EPA.

The 2006 movie *An Inconvenient Truth* won the 2007 Academy Award for Best Documentary Feature. The film, which is narrated by former vice president Al Gore, illustrates the science behind global warming. Gore and Director Davis Guggenheim are pictured here at the Academy Awards in Los Angeles, California, on February 27, 2007.

Democratic congressional leaders also pledged to consider new laws to govern carbon dioxide emissions. In January 2007, Speaker of the House Nancy Pelosi announced the creation of a special committee to produce a global warming bill by July 4. Pelosi stated, "I promise to do everything in my power to achieve energy independence . . . and to stop global warming."[69]

Many in the business community, pressured by investors, also called for more attention to the issue. In January 2007, the United States Climate Action Partnership—a group of the 10 major American corporations, including Alcoa, General Electric, and DuPont—released a report titled *A Call for Action*. It advocated a nationwide limit on carbon dioxide emissions aimed at reducing them as much as 30 percent over a 15-year period. The group timed its report to come out as President Bush delivered his yearly State of the Union address. The speech suggested that even the second Bush administration was ready to acknowledge the threat of global warming. Although the president refused to endorse mandatory caps on emissions, he did, for the first time, admit that global warming is a "serious challenge."[70]

As difficult as this challenge will be, Americans—politicians, industrialists, and average citizens alike—seem increasingly poised to take action. Their new concern suggests that environmentalism is far from dead. Nevertheless, in the years to come, the environmental movement will likely have to change, inventing new ideas, tactics, and methods to deal with problems more complex and dangerous than any that have come before. The survival of the movement—and the survival of our ailing planet—may depend on it.

10

Environmentalism and America

Since Rachel Carson wrote *Silent Spring*, the American environmental movement has grown enormously, if by fits and starts. In the process, it has had an extraordinary effect on life in the United States. Within a single generation, environmentalism has changed the nation's politics, economy, society, and culture. What we eat, where we work, how we spend our leisure time, what we learn in school, who we elect—all have been altered in some way by the environmental movement.

POLITICAL LANDSCAPE

These changes are perhaps most obvious in Washington, D.C. Since 1970, the EPA has become one of the largest agencies in the federal government. It now employs more than 18,000 people. At the same time, the number of laws administered by the EPA has increased, with new legislation proposed each year. These laws naturally have had an effect on the judicial system. Courts—including the Supreme Court—regularly hear lawsuits intended to enforce or challenge environmental laws.

Environmental issues affect not only national politics. State and local politicians must also convince voters they will work to solve environmental problems in their area.

At all levels of government, politicians now often rely on support and campaign funds either from environmental groups seeking new protections or from corporate interests looking to persuade lawmakers to lift established regulations. Although it remains relatively small, the Green Party plays a distinct role in American politics, frequently by highlighting issues that neither the Democratic nor the Republican Party is eager to address.

CHANGING BUSINESS

Environmentalism has also had an obvious impact on business and industry. Energy, mining, timber, and many other industries have had to alter their business practices to adhere to environmental regulations. In the process, they have had to expand their staffs and hire their own teams of environmental scientists, engineers, and lawyers in order to follow (or fight) environmental laws. Many companies also devote considerable time, energy, and funds to public relations campaigns to promote themselves as friends of the environment. These firms realize that Americans, even those who do not consider themselves environmentalists, now frown on corporations identified as polluters.

Similarly, manufacturers know that consumers care if their products have an adverse effect on the environment. For the sake of public relations, companies often voluntarily respond to complaints about their use of excess packaging or potentially toxic substances. For instance, in the 1980s, McDonald's chose to abandon polystyrene hamburger containers, which environmentalists complained were clogging up landfills.

Some entirely new industries, such as pollution control and toxic waste cleanup, have sprung up to help companies obey environmental laws. Others are emerging to address the country's changing energy needs. In anticipation of declining oil supplies and of increasing efforts to combat global warming, companies are developing alternative fuels, such as biodiesel and ethanol, as well as renewable energy sources, including solar and wind power. The energy industry is also investigating the viability of coal-burning power plants that channel emissions safely into underground tunnels instead of releasing them into the air.

The environmental movement itself could be considered a new industry. Many thousands of Americans are employed as environmental experts, lawyers, scientists, lobbyists, and bureaucrats—some working in government, others for private corporations, and still others for environmental groups. In addition, most major newspapers have a reporter assigned to the environmental beat. The Society of Environmental Journalists was founded in 1990, signaling the growth of this new field.

In an effort to find an alternative to oil, many companies are focusing on substitute sources of energy such as solar and wind power. Pictured here is a wind farm in California's Mojave Desert.

LEARNING ABOUT THE ENVIRONMENT

American education also shows the influence of environmentalism. For more than three decades, lessons about environmental concerns have become part of the standard science curricula for almost all elementary and secondary schools. Environmental education tends to focus on practical matters, teaching young people what they can do to be conscientious stewards of the Earth. Because of their constant exposure to these issues in the classroom, many students become environmental monitors at home, overseeing recycling efforts and recommending environmentally friendly products for the household.

At the college level, environmental studies have had an effect on a variety of disciplines—from engineering to psychology to economics. Many new fields have subsequently emerged. For instance, environmental design teaches architects and industrial designers how to make buildings and products that integrate nature with human needs and technological innovations. Environmental history trains students to examine past interactions between humans and the natural world. Environmental philosophy explores the ethical issues surrounding people's relationship with their environment.

Environmental groups have often taken on the role of instructing the general public about environmental issues. They provide members with a steady stream of information through fund-raising drives, publications, and Web sites. For many Americans, membership in an environmental group means that they do little more than write out a check for dues and occasionally leaf through a newsletter. For a few, however, their participation is a vital part of their lives. They might devote the bulk of their free time to an organization by volunteering particular skills, organizing boycotts, writing letters to lawmakers, or taking part in protests.

ENVIRONMENTAL CONSUMERS

Many more Americans, however, prefer to show their interest in the environment in a more passive way—in the choices of the goods they buy. For decades, companies have provided American consumers with a wide variety of environmentally friendly, or ecofriendly, goods. (In general, products are called ecofriendly if their manufacture and use inflict as little harm as possible on living things and on the Earth.)

Some ecofriendly goods appeal to buyers' health fears about toxins and contaminants. Organic foods, for instance, have become far more popular as people have become increasingly concerned about the risks of eating genetically engineered foods, produce treated with chemical pesticides, and meat from animals injected with hormones. Cleaning supplies with natural ingredients have also gained in popularity. Some dry cleaners, too, try to attract customers by using new cleaning methods that do not employ perchloroethylene, a toxic solvent. The cosmetics industry now produces chemical-free goods, advertised both as gentler on the skin and as better for the environment. Many companies also assure consumers that their products are "cruelty free," indicating that ingredients they use have not been tested on animals.

Other ecofriendly goods help to conserve energy and resources. With recent spikes in oil prices, some Americans are trading in their gas-guzzling sport utility vehicles (SUVs) for more fuel-efficient cars. The demand for hybrids, which are powered by a combination of gas and electricity, is also slowly growing. Although they constitute only about one-tenth of 1 percent of all American cars, a 2004 report from the Department of Energy's Oak Ridge National Laboratory predicted hybrids could account for 10 to 15 percent of new car sales by 2012. The use of compact fluorescent lightbulbs, which use less energy than conventional incandescent bulbs, is also on the rise. In 2007, the California legislature, in fact, considered a law banning the sale of traditional bulbs in the state.

Perhaps the most prevalent ecofriendly goods are products made from recycled materials, especially glass, paper, and plastic. By recycling used materials, manufacturers create less waste. Recycled products also require less energy to make.

Because of increased demand for ecofriendly goods, they have become readily available, especially in urban areas. The Internet has made ecoshopping much easier for consumers no matter where they live. At sites such as Ideal Bite (http://idealbite.com), shoppers can find everything from organic chocolate to hormone-free dog food to jackets made from recycled plastic.

The consumer demand for hybrid cars is on the upswing: By 2012, the Department of Energy's Oak Ridge National Laboratory predicts that hybrids could account for up to 10 to 15 percent of new car sales. Here, customers browse the cars on display at the Texas Commission on Environmental Quality's Environmental Trade Show and Conference in May 2006.

GREENING OF THE EVERY DAY

In some ways, environmentalism has become a part of everyday life. For instance, recycling paper and glass, often required by local governments, is an ingrained habit for many Americans. Similarly, people might decide to buy chemical-free cleaning supplies or drive a hybrid car or boycott the products of a notorious corporate polluter. In time, they might become so accustomed to buying one product or avoiding another that they hardly give it a conscious thought.

DANGER AND OPPORTUNITY

In his best-selling book companion to the documentary *An Inconvenient Truth* (2006), former vice president Al Gore outlines the many frightening scenarios that could arise if global warming is left unchecked. However, as he notes in his introduction, "the Chinese expression for 'crisis' consists of two characters side by side. The first is the symbol for 'danger,' the second the symbol for 'opportunity.'"*

In the excerpt below, Gore explains how this idea applies to the crisis of global warming—a danger certainly, but also an opportunity perhaps to change American society for the better:

> The climate crisis is, indeed, extremely dangerous. In fact it is a true planetary emergency. Two thousand scientists, in a hundred countries, working for more than twenty years in the most elaborate and well-organized scientific collaboration in the history of humankind, have forged an exceptionally strong consensus that all the nations on Earth must work together to solve the crisis of global warming....
>
> But along with the danger we face from global warming, this crisis also brings unprecedented opportunities.
>
> What are the opportunities such a crisis also offers? They include not just new jobs and new profits, though there will be plenty of both, we can build clean engines,

Everyday environmentalism is perhaps most clear in the way Americans spend their leisure time. Each weekend, millions visit national and state parks. Even in urban areas, people can "get back to nature"; they can picnic in a city park, walk along a hiking trail, or go bird-watching. Many Americans use their vacation time to camp outdoors, take whale-watching boat tours, or visit an unfamiliar landscape.

This desire to spend time in the natural world has also sparked the ecotourism industry. Ecotourism is popularly

we can harness the Sun and the wind; we can stop wasting energy; we can use our planet's plentiful coal resources without heating the planet.

The procrastinators and deniers would have us believe this will be expensive. But in recent years, dozens of companies have cut emissions of heat-trapping gases while saving money. Some of the world's largest companies are moving aggressively to capture the enormous economic opportunities offered by a clean energy future.

But there's something even more precious to be gained if we do the right thing.

The climate crisis also offers us the chance to experience what very few generations in history have had the privilege of knowing: *a generational mission*; the exhilaration of a compelling *moral purpose*; a shared and unifying *cause*; the thrill of being forced by circumstances to put aside the pettiness and conflict that so often stifle the restless human need for transcendence; *the opportunity to rise*.**

---

* Al Gore, *An Inconvenient Truth: The Planetary Emergency of Global Warming and What We Can Do About It* (Emmaus, Pa.: Rodale Press, 2006).

** Ibid.

used to describe vacations to unsullied environments around the world that are designed to educate tourists about these environments and the local culture. Ecotourism has become a central part of the economy of some countries, including Nepal and Ecuador.

Closer to home, Americans also take in environmental messages through a variety of leisure activities. Magazines such as *National Geographic* and *Audubon* and television documentary programs such as *Nature* and *Nova* present issues to a general audience. Popular songs—from Metallica's "Blackened" to Alabama's "Pass It on Down" to the Dave Matthews Band's "One Sweet World"—also communicate ideas about environmentalism, as do many successful films, including *The Day After Tomorrow* (2004), a fanciful disaster movie about the effects of global warming. Environmental messages are especially common in children's entertainment. *Fern Gully: The Last Rainforest* (1992), *Happy Feet* (2006), and the features of Japanese animator Hayao Miyazaki (including 1984's *Nausicaä of the Valley of the Wind* and 1997's *Princess Mononoke*) are just a few examples.

MOVING FORWARD

Some environmentalists worry that too many Americans are engaged in environmental issues only through their entertainment and consumer choices. After all, watching an environmentally themed movie or buying recycled paper towels may make someone feel good, but it does little to solve the environmental problems the world now faces. As author Benjamin Kline explains in his book *First Along the River*, "[W]e like to think the government's taking care of it and we recycle, buy eco-friendly products, donate to Greenpeace, or simply deny that the crisis exists."[71]

The desire to solve complex problems through easy actions is understandable. In the years to come, however,

Americans may no longer have that luxury. With global warming and oil shortages on the horizon, Americans may have to step up their commitment to environmentalism and make sure their elected officials and business leaders do, as well.

Even more difficult, Americans may have to make major changes in the way they live. They may have to give up big cars that consume huge quantities of gasoline and big houses that require large amounts of energy to heat and cool. They may have to restructure their communities so they do not have to drive as much. They may have to agree to spend tax funds now to avoid payment of the far higher costs—in money, ecological destruction, and human lives—that ignoring our present environmental crisis could result in. Finally, they may have to recognize that these problems will not be solved by individual people or individual countries but instead will require a collective effort by all the citizens of the world. Perhaps, then, Americans can reclaim their role as trailblazers in the struggle to save our Earth.

CHRONOLOGY

1854	Henry David Thoreau's *Walden* is published.
1872	Yellowstone National Park is established.
1892	John Muir founds Sierra Club.
1908	President Theodore Roosevelt hosts Governors' Conference on the Conservation of Natural Resources at the White House.
1913	Congress decides to flood California's Hetch Hetchy Valley over objections of environmentalists.
1933	Civilian Conservation Corps (CCC) is established.
1962	Rachel Carson's *Silent Spring* is published.
1963–64	Congress passes Clean Air Act and Wilderness Act.

Timeline

1892
John Muir founds
Sierra Club

1970
First Earth Day

1872

1973

1872
Yellowstone
National Park
established

1962
Silent Spring
published

1973
Endangered
Species Act

1969	Environmentalists express outrage over oil spill in Santa Barbara Channel and industrial waste fire on Cuyahoga River near Cleveland, Ohio.
1970	U.S. government establishes Environmental Protection Agency; 20 million Americans celebrate first Earth Day.
1971	Keep America Beautiful begins airing iconic "crying Indian" public service announcement.
1973	Congress passes Endangered Species Act.
1974	Federal government responds to Organization of the Petroleum Exporting Countries (OPEC) oil crisis by establishment of a national speed limit of 55 miles per hour.
1979	Greenpeace International is established; accident at Three Mile Island power plant draws attention to nuclear power safety issues.
1980	Congress establishes Superfund to clean up toxic waste dumps; radical environmental group Earth First! is founded.

1983
Secretary of the Interior James Watt and EPA administrator Anne Gorsuch resign

1992
First Earth Summit in Rio de Janeiro, Brazil

2007
Intergovernmental Panel on Climate Change concludes that global warming is "unequivocal" and "very likely" caused by human activity

1983

2007

1989
Exxon Valdez tanker runs aground in Alaska

1997
Kyoto Conference

1983	Secretary of the Interior James Watt and EPA administrator Anne Gorsuch resign amid scandal.
1989	*Time* names "Endangered Earth" the "Planet of the Year"; *Exxon Valdez* runs aground in Alaska, causing massive oil spill; Montreal Protocol calls for ban on ozone-destroying CFCs.
1990	Twentieth anniversary of first Earth Day commemorated in worldwide celebration; spotted owl added to list of endangered species.
1992	World leaders gather in Rio de Janeiro, Brazil, for Earth Summit.
1997	International delegates to Kyoto Conference call for mandatory caps on emissions of carbon dioxide to combat global warming.
2001	President George W. Bush rejects Kyoto Protocol.
2004	"The Death of Environmentalism" initiates debate about future of the environmental movement.
2006	Former vice president Al Gore draws attention to global warming crisis with documentary film *An Inconvenient Truth*.
2007	Report from Intergovernmental Panel on Climate Change concludes that global warming is "unequivocal" and "very likely" caused by human activity.

NOTES

CHAPTER 1

1. Rachel Carson, *Silent Spring,* 1962; repr. (Boston: Houghton Mifflin, 1994), 1.
2. Ibid. 2.
3. Ibid.
4. Ibid.
5. Bruce Watson, "Sounding the Alarm," *Smithsonian* (September 2002): 115.
6. Frank Graham, Jr., "Rachel Carson," *Audubon* (November–December 1998): 83.
7. Watson, "Sounding the Alarm," 116.
8. Ibid.
9. Ibid.
10. Ibid.
11. Peter Matthiessen, "Rachel Carson," *Time* (March 29, 1999): 143.

CHAPTER 2

12. Genesis 1:27–28. (New Revised Standard Version).
13. Benjamin Kline, *First Along the River: A Brief History of the U.S. Environmental Movement,* 2nd ed. (Lanham, Md.: Acada Books, 2000), 20.
14. Stephen E. Whicher, ed., *Selections from Ralph Waldo Emerson* (Boston: Houghton Mifflin, 1957), 24.
15. Kline, *First Along the River,* 47.

CHAPTER 3

16. Frederick Jackson Turner, "The Significance of the Frontier in American History." Available online at *xroads.virginia.edu/~HYPER/TURNER/chapter1.html.*
17. Ibid.
18. Ibid.
19. Kline, *First Along the River,* 54.
20. Ibid.
21. Mark Grossman, *The ABC-CLIO Companion to the Environmental Movement.* (Santa Barbara, Calif.: ABC-CLIO, 1994), 138.
22. Theodore Roosevelt, "John Muir: An Appreciation." Sierra Club. Available online at *http://www.sierraclub.org/john_muir_exhibit/frameindex.html?http://www.sierraclub.org/john_muir_exhibit/life/appreciation_by_roosevelt.html.*

CHAPTER 4

23. Kline, *First Along the River,* 79.
24. Ibid., 77.
25. "The Wilderness Act of 1964." Wilderness.net. Available online at *http://www.wilderness.net/index.cfm?fuse=NWPS&sec=legisAct#2.*

26. Kirkpatrick Sale, *The Green Revolution: The American Environmental Movement 1962–1992* (New York: Hill and Wang, 1993), 17.

CHAPTER 5

27. Philip Shabecoff, *A Fierce Green Fire: The American Environmental Movement* (New York: Hill and Wang, 1993), 113.
28. "The Cities: The Price of Optimism." *Time*, August 1, 1989. Available online at *http://www.time.com/time/magazine/article/0,9171,901182-1,00.html*.
29. Shabecoff, *A Fierce Green Fire*, 118.
30. Ibid., 119.
31. Kline, *First Along the River*, 89.

CHAPTER 6

32. "Richard Nixon: Annual Message to the Congress on the State of the Union, January 22nd, 1970." The American Presidency Project. Available online at *http://www.presidency.ucsb.edu/ws/index.php?pid=2921*.
33. Shabecoff, *A Fierce Green Fire*, 113.
34. Grossman, *The ABC-CLIO Companion to the Environmental Movement*, 90.
35. Ibid.
36. Sale, *The Green Revolution*, 41.
37. Kline, *First Along the River*, 94.

CHAPTER 7

38. Ibid., 101.

39. Sale, *The Green Revolution*, 49.
40. "Dimming Watt." *Time*, October 17, 1983. Available online at *http://www.time.com/time/magazine/printout/0,8816,952189,00.html*.
41. Kline, *First Along the River*, 103.
42. Sale, *The Green Revolution*, 53.

CHAPTER 8

43. Thomas A. Sancton, "What on EARTH Are We Doing?" *Time*, January 2, 1989. Available online at *http://www.time.com/time/magazine/article/0,9171,956627,00.html*.
44. Sale, *The Green Revolution*, 72.
45. Jerome Cramer, "Eco-commercialism: The Selling of the Green." *Time*, September 16, 1991. Available online at *http://www.time.com/time/magazine/article/0,9171,973815,00.html*.
46. Ibid.
47. Kline, *First Along the River*, 105.
48. Ibid., 120.
49. Ibid., 111.
50. Al Gore, *Earth in the Balance* (Boston: Houghton Mifflin, 1992).
51. Kline, *First Along the River*, 130.

CHAPTER 9

52. "U.S. Vice President Al Gore Delivers Acceptance Speech

at Democratic National Convention." CNN.com, August 17, 2000. Available online at *http://www.cnn.com/ELECTION/2000/conventions/democratic/transcripts/gore.html.*

53. Jay Branegan, "Is Al Gore a Hero or a Traitor?" *Time,* April 26, 1999. Available online at *http://www.time.com/time/magazine/article/0,9171,990847,00.html.*

54. David Remnick, "Ozone Man." *The New Yorker*, April 24, 2006. Available online at *http://www.newyorker.com/printables/talk/060424ta_talk_remnick.*

55. Ibid.

56. Ibid.

57. Tracy Watson, "U.S. Joins World on Cause of Warming," *USA Today* (June 4, 2002).

58. "Bush Disses Global Warming Report." CBS News, June 4, 2002. Available online at *http://www.cbsnews.com/stories/2002/06/03/tech/main510920.shtml.*

59. John Heilprin, "EPA Softened Sept. 11 States, Report Finds," *Boston Globe* (August 23, 2003).

60. Michael Shellenberger and Ted Nordhaus, "The Death of Environmentalism: Global Warming Politics in a Post-environmental World." Grist: Environmental News & Commentary. Available online at

http://www.grist.org/news/maindish/2005/01/13/doe-reprint.

61. Ibid.

62. Ibid.

63. Bill McKibben, "Energizing America." Sierra Club. Available online at *http://www.sierraclub.org/sierra/200701/energizing.asp.*

64. Ibid.

65. "Environmentalists Mull Movement's Future," *USA Today* (April 4, 2005).

66. "Group: ExxonMobil Paid to Mislead Public." ABC News, January 3, 2007. Available online at *http://www.abcnews.go.com/Technology/wireStory?id=2767841.*

67. Ian Sample, "Scientists Offered Cash to Dispute Climate Study," *Guardian* (February 2, 2007).

68. Roger Ebert, "An Inconvenient Truth," *Chicago Sun-Times* (June 2, 2006).

69. John Heilprin, "Pelosi Seeks Global Warming Committee." ABC News, January 18, 2007. Available online at *http://www.abcnews.go.com/Politics/wireStory?id=2805623.*

70. "President Bush Delivers State of the Union Address." The White House, January 23, 2007. Available online at *http://www.whitehouse.gov/news/releases/2007/01/20070123-2.html.*

CHAPTER 10

71. Kline, *First Along the River*, 157.

BIBLIOGRAPHY

BOOKS

Barton, Greg, ed. *American Environmentalism*. San Diego: Greenhaven Press, 2002.

Carson, Rachel. *Silent Spring*. 1962. Reprint, Boston: Houghton Mifflin, 1994.

Grossman, Mark. *The ABC-CLIO Companion to the Environmental Movement*. Santa Barbara, Calif.: ABC-CLIO, 1994.

Kline, Benjamin. *First Along the River: A Brief History of the U.S. Environmental Movement*, 2nd ed. Lanham, Md.: Acada Books, 2000.

Sale, Kirkpatrick. *The Green Revolution: The American Environmental Movement, 1962–1992*. New York: Hill and Wang, 1993.

Shabecoff, Philip. *A Fierce Green Fire: The American Environmental Movement*. New York: Hill and Wang, 1993.

Steinberg, Ted. *Down to Earth: Nature's Role in American History*. New York: Oxford University Press, 2002.

WEB SITES

Environmental Protection Agency
http://www.epa.gov

Grist: Environmental News and Commentary
http://www.grist.org

Sierra Club
http://www.sierraclub.org

The Death of Environmentalism: Global Warming Politics in a Post-environmental World
http://www.thebreakthrough.org/images/Death_of_Environmentalism.pdf

***Time* Archive**
http://www.time.com/time/archive

FURTHER READING

BOOKS

Archer, Jules. *To Save the Earth: The American Environmental Movement.* New York: Viking Books, 1998.

Keene, Ann T. *Earthkeepers: Observers and Protectors of Nature.* New York: Oxford University Press, 1994.

Netzley, Patricia D. *Environmental Groups.* San Diego: Lucent Books, 1998.

———. *Issues in the Environment.* San Diego: Lucent Books, 1997.

Pringle, Laurence. *The Environmental Movement.* New York: HarperCollins, 2000.

Sale, Kirkpatrick. *The Green Revolution: The American Environmental Movement, 1962–1992.* New York: Hill and Wang, 1993.

WEB SITES

Environmental Protection Agency
http://www.epa.gov

Greenpeace USA
http://www.greenpeace.org/usa

Grist: Environmental News and Commentary
http://www.grist.org

An Inconvenient Truth
http://www.climatecrisis.net

The Sierra Club
http://www.sierraclub.org

PICTURE CREDITS

INDEX

ABOUT THE CONTRIBUTORS

Author **LIZ SONNEBORN** is a writer living in Brooklyn, New York. A graduate of Swarthmore College, she has written more than 60 books for children and adults, including *The American West*, *A to Z of American Indian Women*, *The Ancient Kushites*, and *Chronology of American Indian History*.

Series editor **TIM McNEESE** is associate professor of history at York College in York, Nebraska, where he is in his fifteenth year of college instruction. Professor McNeese earned an associate of arts degree from York College, a bachelor of arts in history and political science from Harding University, and a master of arts in history from Southern Missouri University. A prolific author of books for elementary, middle and high school, and college readers, McNeese has published more than 80 books and educational materials over the past 20 years, on everything from Picasso to landmark Supreme Court decisions. His writing has earned him a citation in the library reference work *Contemporary Authors*. In 2006, he appeared on the History Channel program *Risk Takers/ History Makers: John Wesley Powell and the Grand Canyon*.